MS Wo
explai

BOOKS AVAILABLE

By both authors:

BP306 A Concise Introduction to Ami Pro 3
BP327 DOS one step at a time
BP337 A Concise User's Guide to Lotus 1-2-3 for Windows
BP341 MS-DOS explained
BP343 A concise introd'n to Microsoft Works for Windows
BP346 Programming in Visual Basic for Windows
BP351 WordPerfect 6 explained
BP352 Excel 5 explained
BP353 WordPerfect 6.0 for Windows explained
BP354 Word 6 for Windows explained
BP362 Access one step at a time
BP372 CA-SuperCalc for Windows explained
BP387 Windows one step at a time
BP388 Why not personalise your PC
BP399 Windows 95 one step at a time*
BP400 Windows 95 explained*
BP402 MS Office one step at a time
BP405 MS Works for Windows 95 explained
BP406 MS Word 95 explained
BP407 Excel 95 explained
BP408 Access 95 one step at a time
BP409 MS Office 95 one step at a time
BP415 Using Netscape on the Internet
BP419 Using Microsoft Explorer on the Internet
BP420 E-mail on the Internet
BP426 MS-Office 97 explained
BP428 MS-Word 97 explained
BP429 MS-Excel 97 explained
BP430 MS-Access 97 one step at a time

By Noel Kantaris:

BP232 A Concise Introduction to MS-DOS
BP258 Learning to Program in C
BP259 A Concise Introduction to UNIX*
BP261 A Concise Introduction to Lotus 1-2-3
BP264 A Concise Advanced User's Guide to MS-DOS
BP274 A Concise Introduction to SuperCalc 5
BP284 Programming in QuickBASIC
BP325 A Concise User's Guide to Windows 3.1

MS Word 95
explained

by

N. Kantaris
and
P.R.M. Oliver

BERNARD BABANI (publishing) LTD.
THE GRAMPIANS
SHEPHERDS BUSH ROAD
LONDON W6 7NF
ENGLAND

PLEASE NOTE

Although every care has been taken with the production of this book to ensure that any projects, designs, modifications and/or programs, etc., contained herewith, operate in a correct and safe manner and also that any components specified are normally available in Great Britain, the Publishers and Author(s) do not accept responsibility in any way for the failure (including fault in design) of any project, design, modification or program to work correctly or to cause damage to any equipment that it may be connected to or used in conjunction with, or in respect of any other damage or injury that may be so caused, nor do the Publishers accept responsibility in any way for the failure to obtain specified components.

Notice is also given that if equipment that is still under warranty is modified in any way or used or connected with home-built equipment then that warranty may be void.

© 1996 BERNARD BABANI (publishing) LTD

First Published – August 1996
Reprinted – December 1997

British Library Cataloguing in Publication Data:

A catalogue record for this book is available from the British Library

ISBN 0 85934 406 1

Cover Design by Gregor Arthur
Cover illustration by Adam Willis
Printed and Bound in Great Britain by Cox & Wyman Ltd, Reading

ABOUT THIS BOOK

MS Word 95 explained has been written for those who want to get to grips with the Microsoft Word for Windows 95 (version 7) word processor and desk top publishing package in the fastest possible time. No previous knowledge is assumed, but the book does not describe how to set up your computer hardware, or how to install and use Windows 95. If you need to know more about the Windows environment, then we suggest you select an appropriate level book for your needs from the 'Books Available' list - the books are graduated in complexity with the less demanding *One step at a time* series, to the more detailed *Explained* series. They are all published by BERNARD BABANI (publishing) Ltd.

This book was written with the busy person in mind. It is not necessary to read several hundred pages covering all there is to know about a subject, when a few selected pages can do the same thing quite adequately! With the help of this book, it is hoped that you will be able to get the most out of Word for Windows and your computer in terms of efficiency, productivity and enjoyment, and that you will be able to do it in the shortest, most effective and informative way.

More emphasis has been placed on an understanding of what we consider to be the critical areas in the program, such as page layout, paragraph styles and the use of frames, than on a general overall description of the package, although we have tried to make the book as complete as possible.

The Word for Windows 95 package is the leading Windows word processor and, we feel, will stand comparison with anything else available today in the marketplace.

If you would like to purchase a Companion Disc for any of the listed books by the same author(s), apart from the ones marked with an asterisk, containing the file/program listings which appear in them, then fill in the form at the back of the book and send it to Phil Oliver at the stipulated address.

ABOUT THE AUTHORS

Noel Kantaris graduated in Electrical Engineering at Bristol University and after spending three years in the Electronics Industry in London, took up a Tutorship in Physics at the University of Queensland. Research interests in Ionospheric Physics, led to the degrees of M.E. in Electronics and Ph.D. in Physics. On return to the UK, he took up a Post-Doctoral Research Fellowship in Radio Physics at the University of Leicester, and then in 1973 a lecturing position in Engineering at the Camborne School of Mines, Cornwall, (part of Exeter University), where since 1978 he has also assumed the responsibility for the Computing Department.

Phil Oliver graduated in Mining Engineering at Camborne School of Mines in 1967 and since then has specialised in most aspects of surface mining technology, with a particular emphasis on computer related techniques. He has worked in Guyana, Canada, several Middle Eastern countries, South Africa and the United Kingdom, on such diverse projects as: the planning and management of bauxite, iron, gold and coal mines; rock excavation contracting in the UK; international mining equipment sales and technical back up and international mine consulting for a major mining house in South Africa. In 1988 he took up a lecturing position at Camborne School of Mines (part of Exeter University) in Surface Mining and Management.

ACKNOWLEDGEMENTS

We would like to thank the staff of Text 100 Limited for providing the software programs on which this work was based. We would also like to thank colleagues at the Camborne School of Mines for the helpful tips and suggestions which assisted us in the writing of this book.

TRADEMARKS

CONTENTS

1. PACKAGE OVERVIEW

Microsoft's Word for Windows 95 is the best selling Windows word processor and is fully integrated with Microsoft Office 95. In all the Windows versions Word has had a leaning towards desk top publishing which offers fully editable WYSIWYG (what you see is what you get) modes that can be viewed in various zoom levels, including full page. Couple this with the ability to include and manipulate full colour graphics and you can see the enormous power of the program. Once you have overcome the first hurdle and started to use Word 7 for Windows 95, you will find it both intuitive and an easy program to produce the type of word processed output you would not have dreamt possible.

Word, in common with all other MS Office 95 applications, makes use of what is known as IntelliSense, which anticipates what you want to do and produces the correct result. For example, AutoCorrect and AutoFormat can, when activated, correct common spelling mistakes and format an entire document automatically. Other Wizards can help you with everyday tasks and/or make complex tasks easier to manage.

With OfficeLinks and OLE (Object Linking and Embedding), you can move and share information seamlessly between MS Office 95 applications. For example, you can drag information from one application to another, and can insert a Microsoft Excel worksheet directly into a Word document by simply clicking a button on a Word toolbar.

Finally, Microsoft Visual Basic for Applications, gives you a powerful and flexible development platform with which to create custom solutions.

Hardware and Software Requirements

If Microsoft Word is already installed on your computer, you can safely skip the rest of this chapter.

To install and use MS Word, you need an IBM-compatible PC equipped with Intel's 80386sx (or higher) processor. We recommend a minimum processor speed of 33 megahertz (MHz). In addition, you need the following:

- Windows 95, Windows NT or Windows NT Advanced Server version.

- Random access memory (RAM): 4MB; 8MB recommended when running more than one MS Office program.

- Hard disc space available for MS Word 95: 12.5MB for Word and 3 MB for converters, filters, and data access tools.

- Video adapter: VGA or higher resolution. If you are embedding colour pictures, you will need a 256-colour video adapter.

- Pointing device: Microsoft Mouse or compatible.

Realistically, to run Microsoft Word for Windows 95 with reasonable sized applications, you will need a 486 or a Pentium PC with at least 8MB of RAM. To run Microsoft Word 95 from a network, you must also have a network compatible with your Windows operating environment, such as Microsoft's Windows 95, Windows NT, LAN Manager, or Novell's NetWare.

Although it is possible to operate from the keyboard alone, the availability of a mouse is a must if you are going to benefit from the program's features and from Window's Graphical User Interface (GUI). After all, pointing and clicking at an option on the screen, is a lot easier than having to learn several different key combinations. So, if you can, install a mouse.

2

Major Word Features

Some of the major features Word for Windows 95 contains, include the ability to:

- Drag and drop when editing text, tables, and graphics in a document and across windows - this is more convenient than cutting and pasting.

- Shortcut menus relevant to the type of work you are carrying out at the time, to help speed your work.

- Create documents that have different formatting, multiple columns, and a variety of page layouts.

- Add comments and annotations to a document without changing the original text.

- Use revision marks so that intended changes can be seen easily - such changes can then be accepted or rejected.

- Create a glossary of text and graphics which can be inserted in any part of a document.

- Insert footnotes in any part of a document's page with automatic numbering.

- AutoCorrect which fixes common typing errors as you work, and AutoText which speeds up the addition of frequently used text, tables, lists, and graphics, into your document.

- Correct your spelling with an extensive spell checker - you can even add special words to it.

- Check a document's grammar and style and customise the latter to suit your needs.

- Look up the meaning of words and find synonyms with the use of the thesaurus.

- Create tables in a document automatically, which can contain text, numbers, pictures and objects - formatting can be applied to the whole, or individual parts of it.

- Add pictures created in another application to a document, scale them proportionally, or crop them to requirement.

- Ability to create objects, such as graphs, charts and equations, which can be modified, edited, moved and/or copied.

- Insert a frame around a paragraph, picture or object, then move the frame and its contents, or change its size.

- Use the Bullets and Numbering command which can easily add bullets and numbers to multiple-level lists.

- Use the Heading Numbering command which can create numbered headings with built-in heading styles.

- AutoCaption which helps you to quickly add captions and create cross-references to captions, headings, tables, and other items.

- View documents in a variety of ways, preview a document before printing, print a document or print/view information about a document.

- Full screen view ability to maximise the text area on your screen by hiding menus, toolbars, and rulers.

- Automated printing of envelopes, provided the printer's envelope feeder has been installed.

- Transparently import existing files produced by most versions of Microsoft and WordPerfect word processors, as well as worksheets and databases produced in Excel, Lotus 1-2-3, and dBase formats.

- Link and embed information or objects (OLE) created in other Windows applications into a Word document.

- Use the optional user's help to ease the change from WordPerfect to Word for Windows.

- Network the program so users can share information.

New Features in Word:
Word for Windows 95 has many new features over and above those found in previous versions of the program. These include:

- The ability to automatically format a document as you type. Typing three or more consecutive hyphens (-) and pressing <Enter> creates a thin line border, while typing three or more consecutive equal signs (=) and pressing <Enter> creates a double-line border.

- The ability to automatically apply a built-in heading style to text as you type. Typing a line of text and pressing <Enter> twice, causes Word to apply Heading 1 style to the text, while starting a line with a tab, results in Heading 2 style.

- The ability to automatically change ordinary numbers and fractions you type in to make them easier to read, as shown here.

You type	Word changes the format to
1st	1st
2nd	2nd
1/2	½

- The ability to automatically create numbered or bulleted lists. For example, starting a list with a number or an asterisk followed by punctuation (such as a period), causes Word to insert a number bullet in front of each line in the list, until the list is completed.

- The ability to automatically correct text and replace a number of key presses with particular symbols, as shown to the right.

You type	Word inserts
:)	☺
:(	☹
<--	←
-->	→
<==	⇐
==>	⇒
<=>	⇔
(c)	©
(TM)	™

- The ability to automatically keep track of many words you do not want the AutoCorrect feature to change. For example, typing MB or MHz will cause AutoCorrect to change these to Mb and Mhz. However, using the Undo feature to change such words to their original look, causes Word to note the reversal and to avoid 'correcting' such words in the future.

5

- The ability to open or find documents by simply clicking the Open option on the File menu.

- The ability to see the contents of documents without opening them. To preview a document, select it and click the Preview button.

- The ability to manage a document from within the Open dialogue box. Right-clicking a document opens a shortcut menu, shown here, to help you with appropriate house-keeping functions.

- The ability to find and replace all word forms easily. For example, replacing the word 'produce' with 'create' will also replace 'producing' with 'creating' and 'produces' with 'creates'.

- The ability to check your spelling while you type. If a word is not in the dictionary, Word marks it with a wavy red line. To select from a list of spelling choices, right-click the marked word.

- The ability to choose from three built-in families of templates; contemporary, elegant, and professional. Choosing one of these, can help you create a consistent look for your document.

- The ability to mark text with a highlighter, so that it is easier to emphasise important parts of a message. To mark text, select it and click the Highlight button, shown here, and select the colour you want to use from the displayed list.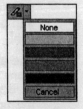

- The ability of the new TipWizard to track your actions and suggest better ways to complete your tasks.

In addition, if you have Microsoft Exchange on your computer and have elected to use Word as an e-mail editor when installing it, then you can use Word's advanced editing and formatting features when you work with electronic mail.

6

Installing Word

Installing Word on your computer's hard disc is made very easy with the use of the SETUP program, which even configures Word automatically to take advantage of the computer's hardware.

If you are installing from floppy discs, insert the first Setup disc (Disc 1) in the A: drive, or if you are installing from a CD-ROM, insert the CD in the CD-ROM drive. If you are installing from a network drive, make a note of the drive letter because you will need it later. Then do the following:

- Click the **Start** button on the Windows 95 Taskbar and select **Settings, Control Panel**.

- On the displayed Control Panel window, double-click the Add/Remove Programs icon, shown here.

- On the Add/Remove Programs Properties dialogue box, click the Install/Uninstall tab and press the **Install** button.

- SETUP will scan your disc for already installed parts of Microsoft Office and will advise you as to the folder in which you should install Word. This will most likely be **Msoffice** - we suggest you accept all the default options.

- Follow the SETUP instructions on the screen, until the installation of Microsoft Word program files starts.

- When a new disc is required (if you are installing from floppy discs), the installation program will inform you by displaying an appropriate dialogue box.

When all discs have been read, the SETUP program will modify your system files automatically so that you can start Word easily by creating and displaying a new entry in the **Start, Programs** cascade menu, with the icon shown here. Clicking this menu entry will start Microsoft Word.

If you have MS-Office installed, SETUP also adds Word to the Microsoft Shortcut Bar facility (see next page).

The Office Shortcut Bar:

The Microsoft Office Shortcut Bar, provides a convenient way to work with your documents and the Office applications (including Microsoft Word) by complementing the Windows 95 **Start** menu.

The various icons on the Shortcut Bar, shown below, have the following function:

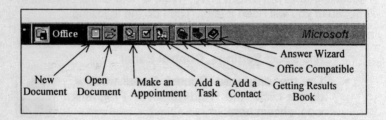

The Start a New Document button: Allows you to select in the displayed dialogue box the tab containing the type of document you want to work with. Double-clicking the type of document or template you want, automatically loads the appropriate application.

The Open a Document button: Allows you to work with an existing document. Opening a document, first starts the application originally used to create it.

The Schedule buttons: Allow you to schedule an appointment, schedule a task, and add a contact name.

Getting Results Book button: Provides you with suggestions on how to work efficiently with the Microsoft Office applications.

Office Compatible button: Provides demonstrations on applications which are compatible with Microsoft Office.

Answer Wizard button: Provides help on various topics which you might need while working with Office.

The Mouse Pointers

In Microsoft Word, as with all other graphical based programs, the use of a mouse makes many operations both easier and more fun to carry out.

Word makes use of the mouse pointers available in Windows 95, some of the most common of which are illustrated below. When Word is initially started up the first you will see is the hourglass, which turns into an upward pointing hollow arrow once the application screen appears on your display. Other shapes depend on the type of work you are doing at the time.

The hourglass which displays when you are waiting while performing a function.

The arrow which appears when the pointer is placed over menus, scrolling bars, and buttons.

The I-beam which appears in normal text areas of the screen.

The large 4-headed arrow which appears after choosing the **Control, Move/Size** command(s) for moving or sizing windows.

The double arrows which appear when over the border of a window, used to drag the side and alter the size of the window.

The Help hand which appears in the Help windows, and is used to access 'hypertext' type links.

Microsoft Word, like the rest of the Microsoft Office applications and other Windows packages, have additional mouse pointers which facilitate the execution of selected commands. Some of these, shown on the next page, have the following functions:

9

↓   The vertical pointer which appears when pointing over a column in a table and used to select the column.

➡   The horizontal pointer which appears when pointing at a row in a table and used to select the row.

⇗   The slanted arrow which appears when the pointer is placed in the selection bar area of text or a table.

↔‖↔   The vertical split arrow which appears when pointing over the area separating two columns in a table and used to size a column.

⇕   The horizontal split arrow which appears when pointing over the split box area of the screen.

+   The frame cross which you drag to create a frame.

✐   The draw pointer which appears when you are drawing freehand.

Word has a few additional mouse pointers to the ones above, but their shape is mostly self-evident.

Some Word operations display a '?' button on the right end of their dialogue box or window, as shown here. Clicking this button changes the mouse pointer from its usual inclined arrow shape to the 'What's this?' shape. Pointing to an object in the dialogue box or window and clicking, opens a Help topic.

10

2. THE WORD ENVIRONMENT

Starting the Program

Word is started in Windows 95 either by clicking the **Start** button then selecting **Program** and clicking on the 'Microsoft Word' icon on the cascade menu, or by clicking the 'Open a Document' icon on the Office Shortcut Bar and double-clicking on a Word document file. In the latter case the document will be loaded into Word at the same time.

The first time you use Word you get the 'What's New' Help screen displayed. After that, to get back to this Help screen, use **Help, Answer Wizard** and type *what's new* in the Type Your Request box, then select What's New in Microsoft Word 95. We suggest you spend a little time examining at least the first three options of this Help screen.

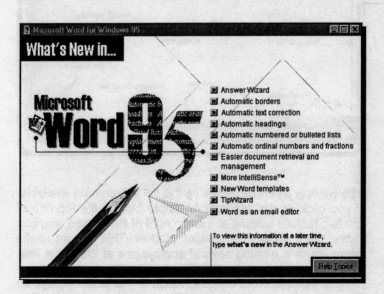

The Word Screen

The opening 'blank' screen of Word for Windows 95 is shown below. It is perhaps worth spending some time looking at the various parts that make up this screen. Word follows the usual Microsoft Windows 95 conventions and if you are familiar with these you can skip through this section. Otherwise a few minutes might be well spent here.

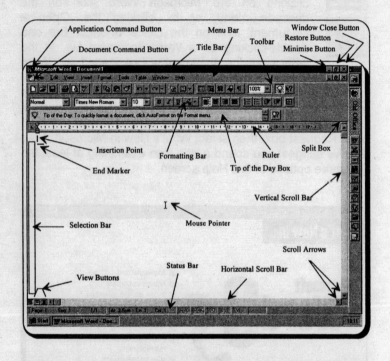

The window as shown takes up the full screen area available. If you click on the application restore button, the top one of the two restore buttons at the top right of the screen, you can make Word show in a smaller window. This can be useful when you are running several applications at the same time and you want to transfer between them with the mouse.

Note that the Word window, which in this case displays an empty document with the title 'Document1', has a solid 'Title bar', indicating that it is the active application window.

Although multiple windows can be displayed simultaneously, you can only enter data into the active window (which will always be displayed on top). Title bars of non active windows appear a lighter shade than that of the active one.

The Word screen is divided into several areas which have the following functions:

Area	*Function*
Command buttons	Clicking on the top command button, (see upper-left corner of Word's window), displays a pull-down menu which can be used to control the program window. It includes commands for restoring, moving, sizing, maximising, minimising, and closing the window. The lower command button controls the document window in the same manner.
Title Bar	The bar at the top of a window which displays the application name and the name of the current document.
Minimise Button	When clicked on, this button minimises the application to the Windows Taskbar, or a document to an icon.
Restore Button	When clicked on, this button restores the active window to the position and size that was occupied before it was maximised. The restore button is then replaced by a Maximise button, as shown here, which is used to set the window to full screen size.

Close button	The extreme top right button that you click to close a window.
Menu Bar	The bar below the Title bar which allows you to choose from several menu options. Clicking on a menu item displays the pull-down menu associated with that item.
Toolbar	The bar below the Menu bar which contains buttons that give you mouse click access to the functions most often used in the program (see Appendix A). These are grouped according to function.
Formatting Bar	The buttons on this bar allow you to change the attributes of a font, such as italic and underline, and also to format text in various ways. The Formatting Bar contains three boxes; a style box, a font box and a size box which show which style, font and size of characters are currently being used. These boxes give access to other installed styles, fonts and character sizes.
Ruler	The area where you can see and set tabulation points and indents.
Split Box	The area above the top vertical scroll button which when dragged allows you to split the screen.
Scroll Bars	The areas on the screen (extreme right and bottom of each window) that contain scroll boxes in vertical and horizontal bars. Clicking on these bars allows you to control the part of a document which is visible on the screen.

Scroll Arrows	The arrowheads at each end of each scroll bar at which you can click to scroll the screen up and down one line, or left and right 10% of the screen, at a time.
Selection Bar	The area on the screen in the left margin of the Word window (marked here with a box for convenience), where the mouse pointer changes to an arrow that slants to the right. Clicking the left mouse button once selects the current line, while clicking twice selects the current paragraph.
Insertion pointer	The pointer used to specify the place of text insertion.
Views Buttons	Clicking these buttons changes screen views quickly.
Status Bar	The bottom line of the document window that displays status information, and in which a short help description appears when you point and click on a button.

The Menu Bar Options:

Each menu bar option has associated with it a pull-down sub-menu. To activate the menu, either press the <Alt> key, which causes the first option of the menu (in this case the Document Control Menu box) to be selected, then use the right and left arrow keys to highlight any of the options in the menu, or use the mouse to point to an option. Pressing either the <Enter> key, or the left mouse button, reveals the pull-down sub-menu of the highlighted menu option. The sub-menu of the **File** option is shown on the next page.

Menu options can also be activated directly by pressing the <Alt> key followed by the underlined letter of the required option. Thus, pressing <Alt+F>, causes the pull-down **File** sub-menu to be displayed. You can use the up and down arrow keys to move the highlighted bar up and down a

15

sub-menu, or the right and left arrow keys to move along the options in the menu bar. Note that as you move up and down a sub-menu the status bar shows a brief description of the highlighted option. Pressing the <Enter> key selects the highlighted option or executes the highlighted command. Pressing the <Esc> key once, closes the pull-down sub-menu, while pressing the <Esc> key for a second time, closes the menu system.

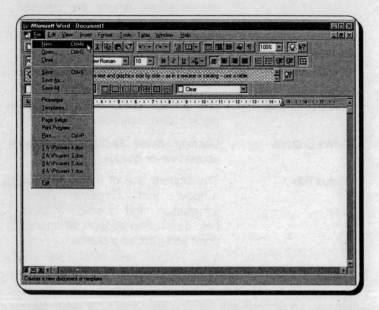

Some of the sub-menu options can be accessed with 'quick key' combinations from the keyboard. Such combinations are shown on the drop-down menus, for example, <Ctrl+S> is the quick key for the **Save** option in the **File** sub-menu. If a sub-menu option is not available, at any time, it will display in a grey colour. Some menu options only appear in Word when that tool is being used, but the ones described on the next page remain constant.

The following is a brief description of the standard menu options. For a more detailed description of each sub-menu item, either highlight it and read the text on the status bar, or use the on-line **Help** system, described later.

File   Produces a pull-down menu of mainly file related tasks, such as creating a **New** document, the ability to **Open**, or **Close** files, and **Save** files with the same name, or **Save As** a different name. You can view a specific file's **Properties**, and change the **Template** or its options. Finally, you can use **Page Setup** to set the margins and the size of your printed page, **Print Preview** a document on screen before committing it to paper, **Print** a document and select your current printer, and also **Exit** the program. This sub-menu also displays the last four documents you used so that you can open them easily.

Edit   Produces a pull-down menu which allows you to **Undo** changes made, **Cut**, **Copy** and **Paste** text and graphics, **Find** specific text in a document, **Find & Replace** text, jump to any location in a document, insert or define **AutoText** items of frequently used text or graphics, assign a name (**Bookmark**) to a section of your document, view and update **Links**, or open a selected **Object**.

View   Produces a pull-down menu which contains screen display options which allow you to change the editing view to **Normal** or **Outline**, display the page in **Page Layout** (WYSIWYG - what you see is what you get), or switch to **Master Document** mode (a document that takes some or all of its contents from one or more Word documents), control whether a **Full Screen** is displayed and whether the **Toolbars**, or **Ruler** are displayed, show a list of **Headers/Footers**, open windows for viewing **Footnotes**, or **Annotations**, and determine the scale of the editing view by using the **Zoom** option.

Insert   Produces a pull-down menu which allows you to insert **Breaks** to ends of pages, columns, or sections, add **Page Numbers** to a document, insert a comment and activate the **Annotation** pane. You can also insert the **Date and Time** into a document, a **Field** (instruction) for computed contents, special characters with **Symbol**, or a new **Form Field**, at the cursor position. In addition you can insert a **Footnote** reference, place a **Caption** above or below a selected object, or a **Cross-reference**. The **Index and Tables** option allows you to build an index entry, an index, or tables of contents, tables, etc. Finally, you can insert the contents of a **File**, an empty **Frame** (or frame selected text), a **Picture**, or an **Object** into the active document.

Format   Produces a pull-down menu which allows you to alter the appearance of text, both on the screen and when printed. Such features as font, size, colour, alignment, print spacing, justification, and enhancements (bold, underlined and italic) are included. You can change the indent and spacing of a selected **Paragraph**, set and clear **Tabs**, or change the **Border and Shading** of a selected paragraph, table cell(s), or picture. You can also change the **Columns** format of the selected section, **Change Case**, format the first character of a paragraph as a **Drop Cap**(ital), create bullet or number lists and change the numbering options for heading level styles. You can further select options to **AutoFormat** a document, browse and apply or modify **Styles**, set the properties of a **Frame**, or change the scaling and size of a **Picture**, or change the fill, line, size and position of a selected **Drawing Object**.

Tools   Produces a pull-down menu that gives access to the **Spelling** checker, the **Thesaurus**, and the **Hyphenation** option. It is from here that you can change the **Language** formatting of the selected characters, display the **Word Count** statistics of the current document, add or delete **AutoCorrect** entries, prepare for **Mail Merge**, or create and print **Envelopes and Labels**. Further, you can set **Revision** marking for the active document, and run, create, delete or revise a **Macro** (a set of instructions). Finally, you can **Customize** Word to your requirements and you can change various categories of Word for Windows **Options**.

Table   You can use the **Insert Table** option of the pull-down menu to create a table of specified rows and columns at the insertion point. Once a table exists, the rest of the options of the pull-down menu become available to you. From here you can **Insert Rows**, **Delete**, **Merge** and **Split Cells**, **Select** a **Row**, a **Column** or a **Table.** Further, you can select the **Table AutoFormat** option to choose from a set of pre-formatted table styles and have them applied to your table, change the **Cell Height and Width**, and toggle the table **Headings** attribute on and off. Finally, you can select a section of text and use the **Convert Text to Table** option to have it incorporated within a table, rearrange a selection into a specified **Sort** order, insert a paragraph mark above the current table row by using the **Split Table** option, insert a **Formula** in a cell, and toggle the table **Gridlines** on and off.

Window	Produces a menu to open a **New Window**, and control the display of existing open windows on the screen.
Help	Activates the help menu which you can use to access the **Microsoft Word Help Topics**, or the **Answer Wizard**, or **The Microsoft Network** (if you have installed it and are connected), or get **WordPerfect** user help and information on **Technical Support**.

Shortcut Menus:

New to this and the previous version of Word are context-sensitive shortcut menus. If you click the right mouse button on any screen, or document, a shortcut menu is displayed with the most frequently used commands relating to the type of work you were doing at the time.

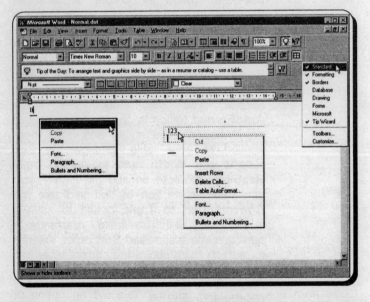

The composite screen dump above shows in turn the shortcut menus that open when the editing area is selected, a table is selected, or either of the Toolbars is selected.

So, whatever you are doing in Word, you have rapid access to a menu of relevant functions by right clicking your mouse. Left clicking the mouse at a menu selection will choose that function.

Dialogue Boxes:

Three periods after a sub-menu option or command, means that a dialogue box will open when the option or command is selected. A dialogue box is used for the insertion of additional information, such as the name of a file or path.

To see a dialogue box, press <Alt+F>, and select the **Open** option. The 'Open' dialogue box is displayed.

When a dialogue box opens, the easiest way to move around it is by clicking with the mouse, otherwise the <Tab> key can be used to move the cursor from one column in the box to another (<Shift+Tab> moves the cursor backwards). Alternatively you can move directly to a desired field by holding the <Alt> key down and pressing the underlined letter in the field name.

Within a column of options you must use the arrow keys to move from one to another. Having selected an option or typed in information, you must press a command button such as the **OK** or **Cancel** button, or choose from additional options.

To select the **OK** button with the mouse, simply point and click, while with the keyboard you must first press the <Tab> key until the dotted rectangle moves to the required button, and then press the <Enter> key. Pressing <Enter> at any time while a dialogue box is open, will cause the marked items to be selected and the box to be closed.

Some dialogue boxes contain List boxes which show a column of available choices (similar to the one at the bottom of the previous screen dump which appeared by pressing the down-arrow button). If there are more choices than can be seen in the area provided, use the scroll bars to reveal them. To select a single item from a List box, either double-click the item, or use the arrow keys to highlight the item and press <Enter>. Other dialogue boxes contain Option buttons with a list of mutually exclusive items. The default choice is marked with a black dot against its name, while unavailable options are dimmed. Other dialogue boxes contain Check boxes which offer a list of options you can switch on or off. Selected options show a cross in the box against the option name.

To cancel a dialogue box, either press the **Cancel** button, or press the <Esc> key. Pressing the <Esc> key in succession, closes one dialogue box at a time, and eventually aborts the menu option.

The Formatting Bar:

This is located below the Toolbar at the top of the Word for Windows screen and is divided into seven sections, as shown below. These can only be accessed by clicking on them with the left mouse button.

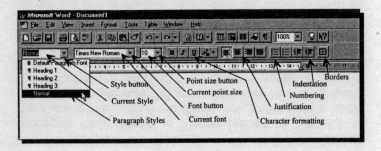

The Current Style box on the left of the Character formatting buttons, shows the style of the current paragraph; the one containing the cursor. By clicking the down-arrow button next to it, a list of all the available styles in the active template is produced (as shown). Clicking on one of these will change the style of the current paragraph.

To the right of the Style button is the Current font box which shows the current typeface. Clicking on the down-arrow button to the right of it allows you to change the typeface of any selected text. The Current point size box shows the size of selected characters. This size can be changed by clicking on the down-arrow button next to it and selecting another size from the displayed list.

Next, are four Character formatting buttons which allow you to enhance selected text by emboldening, italicising, underlining, or colour highlighting it. The next four buttons allow you to change the justification of a selected paragraph, and the next four help you set the different types of Numbering and· Indentation options. The last button allows you to add borders and shading to selected paragraphs, table cells and frames.

The Status Bar:

This is located at the bottom of the Word window and is used to display statistics about the active document.

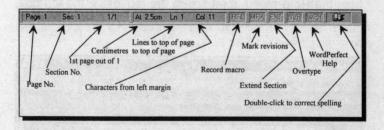

For example, when a document is being opened, the Status bar displays for a short time its name and length in terms of total number of characters. Once a document is opened, the Status bar displays the statistics of the document at the insertion point; here it is on Page 1, Section 1, 11 characters from the left margin.

23

Double-clicking the left of the status bar displays the Go To dialogue box, and double-clicking the other features will activate them. There is even help for WordPerfect users converting to Word. To activate this facility, double-click on **WPH**, or to make it 'permanent' use the **Help** command, select **WordPerfect Help,** click the **Options** button in the displayed dialogue box, and check the **Help for WordPerfect Users** box.

Note: If you do not need to have the **Help for WordPerfect Users** permanently available to you, it is a good idea not to set this option as it can have an adverse effect on the way you work. For example, if the WordPerfect Users help is switched on, you cannot delete sections of your document by highlighting them and pressing the <Del> key. We find this extremely annoying. Another annoying feature we found is that you will have to specify hanging indents separately for each paragraph without being able to carry the formatting from the first paragraph to the rest by simply pressing the <Enter> key. The list does not end with these two examples; there are many more!

Using Help in Word
Using the Microsoft Windows Help Program, Word provides on-line Help for every function. One way of obtaining help on a specific topic is to select the Answer Wizard, by selecting it from the **Help** menu, then typing the request in the top box, as follows:

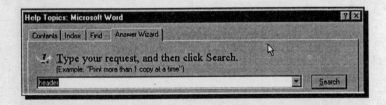

Pressing the **Search** button, lists the following information in the second box:

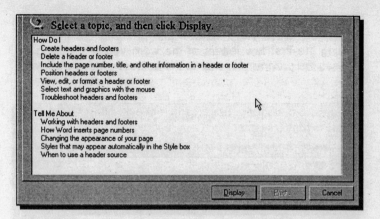

Another way is to use the **Help, Microsoft Word Help Topics** command, then click the Contents tab, to obtain the following:

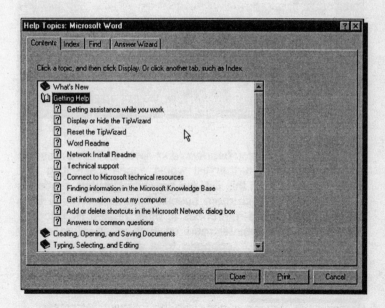

Help topics can be printed on paper by selecting the topic, then clicking the **Print** button.

Further help can be obtained by selecting **Help**, then the **Microsoft Word Help Topics** and pressing the Index tab. Typing the first few letters of the word you are looking for, causes the program to jump to the nearest word, as follows:

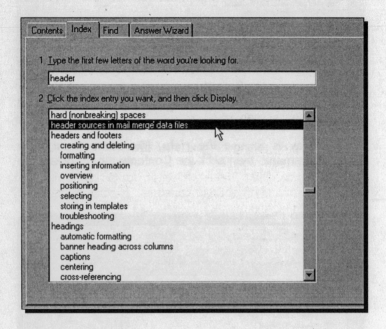

If you were to select *headers and footers*, then press the **Display** button, a further list would appear. Selecting *Add page numbers* from this list and pressing **Display**, produces a further window with more specific information. Many Help topics contain cross-references to other related Help topics. When the mouse pointer rests on such cross-references, it changes to a pointing hand. These are often known as 'hypertext' links, and clicking the hand pointer on them displays further information.

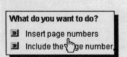

The Find tab on the **Microsoft Word Help Topics** window works in the same way as the Index tab.

In addition, there are several ways to obtain on-line Help. These are:

On-line Help Messages: Word displays a command description in the Status bar when you choose a menu or command.

Context Sensitive Help: Simply press **F1** to get instant help on any menu function or formatting action that you are carrying out. If you are not using a menu box you will bring up the Answer Wizard. Pressing <Esc>, or clicking the **Cancel** button, will close the Answer Wizard and return you to your original screen.

Another way of getting context sensitive help is to click the Help button on the Toolbar, shown here, then move the modified mouse pointer to an area of the document or onto a particular Toolbar button and press the left mouse button.

3. WORD DOCUMENT BASICS

When the program is first used, all Word's features default to those shown on page 12. It is quite possible to use Word in this mode, without changing any main settings, but obviously it is possible to customise the package to your exact needs, as we shall see later.

Entering Text

In order to illustrate some of Word's capabilities, you need to have a short text at hand. We suggest you type the memo displayed below into a new document. At this stage, don't worry if the length of the lines below differ from those on your display.

As you type in text, any time you want to force a new line, or paragraph, just press <Enter>. While typing within a paragraph, Word sorts out line lengths automatically (known as 'word wrap'), without you having to press any keys to move to a new line. If you make a mistake while typing, press the <BkSp> key enough times to erase the mistake and start again.

MEMO TO PC USERS

Networked Computers

The microcomputers in the Data Processing room are a mixture of IBM compatible PCs with either 486 or Pentium processors. They all have 3.5" floppy drives of 1.44MB capacity, and some also have CD-ROM drives. The PCs are connected to various printers via a network; the Laser printers available giving best output.

The computer you are using will have at least a 540MB capacity hard disc on which a number of software programs, including the latest version of Windows, have been installed. To make life easier, the hard disc is highly structured with each program installed in a separate folder (directory).

Moving Around a Document

You can move the cursor around a document with the normal direction keys, and with the key combinations listed below.

To move	*Press*
Left one character	←
Right one character	→
Up one line	↑
Down one line	↓
Left one word	Ctrl+←
Right one word	Ctrl+→
To beginning of line	Home
To end of line	End
To paragraph beginning	Ctrl+↑
To paragraph end	Ctrl+↓
Up one screen	PgUp
Down one screen	PgDn
To top of previous page	Ctrl+PgUp
To top of next page	Ctrl+PgDn
To beginning of file	Ctrl+Home
To end of file	Ctrl+End

In a multi-page document, use the **Edit**, **Go To** command (or <Ctrl+G>), to jump to a specified page number.

Obviously, you need to become familiar with the above methods of moving the cursor around a document (see also Appendix B), particularly if you are not using a mouse and you spot an error in a document which needs to be corrected, which is the subject of the next chapter.

Templates and Paragraph Styles

When you start Word for the first time, the Style Status box (at the extreme left of the Formatting bar) contains the word **Normal**. This means that all the text you have entered, at the moment, is shown in the Normal paragraph style which is one of the styles available in the NORMAL template. Every document produced by Word has to use a template, and NORMAL is the default. A template contains, both the document page settings and a set of formatting instructions which can be applied to text.

Changing Paragraph Styles:

To change the style of a paragraph, do the following:

- Place the cursor (insertion pointer) on the paragraph in question, say the title line

- Left click the Style Status button, and select the **Heading 1** style.

The selected paragraph reformats instantly in bold, and in Arial typeface of point size 14.

With the cursor in the second line of text, select **Heading 3** which reformats the line in Arial 12. Your memo should now look presentable, as shown below.

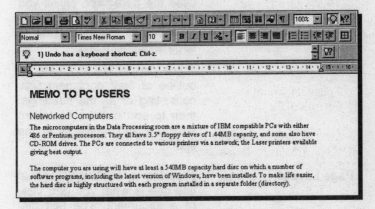

Document Screen Displays

Word provides four display modes, Normal, Outline, Page Layout, and Master Document, as well as the options to view your documents in a whole range of screen enlargements by

selecting **Zoom**. You control all these viewing options with the **View** sub-menu, shown here, and when a document is displayed you can switch freely between them. When first loaded the screen displays in Normal mode.

The mode options have the following effect, and some can also be accessed by clicking the View buttons on the left of the Status bar.

Normal

Returns you to normal viewing from either Outline or Page Layout viewing mode.

Outline

Provides a collapsible view of a document, which enables you to see its organisation at a glance. You can display all the text in a file, or just the text that uses the paragraph styles you specify. Using this mode, allows you to quickly rearrange large sections of text.

Some people like to create an outline of their document first, consisting of all the headings, then to sort out the document structure and finally fill in the text.

Page Layout

Provides a WYSIWYG (what you see is what you get) view of a document. The text displays in the typefaces and point sizes you specify, and with the selected attributes (alignment, indentation, spacing, etc.). All frames, tables, graphics, headers, footers, and footnotes appear on the screen as they will in the final printed document.

Master Document

Provides you with an outline view of a document that takes its contents from one or more Word documents.

For example, each chapter of a book could be made into a sub-document of such a Master Document. The Master Document could then be used to re-organise, add or remove sub-documents. Selecting this mode, causes Word to display the Master Document and Outline toolbars.

Full Screen

Presents you with a clean, un-cluttered screen; the Toolbars, Ruler, Scroll bars, and Status bar are removed. To return to the usual screen, click the 'Full' icon, shown here, which appears at the bottom of your screen when in this mode.

Zoom

Allows you to change the viewing magnification factor from its default value of 100%. This can also be changed by clicking the 'Zoom Control' icon on the Toolbar. Clicking its down arrow button, reveals other mag- nification factors, as shown here.

Changing Default Options

Modifying Margins:

To change the standard page margins for your entire document from the cursor position onward, or for selected text (more about this later), do the following:

- Select the **File, Page Setup** command

- Click the left mouse button at the **Margins** tab on the displayed dialogue box, shown below.

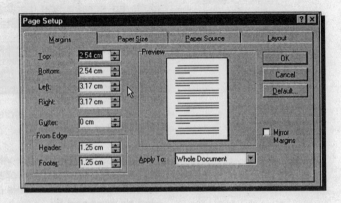

The 'Preview' page in the middle of the box shows how your changes will look on a real page.

Changing the Default Paper Size:

To change the default paper size from the size set during installation to a different size, do the following:

- Select the **File, Page Setup** command

- Click the left mouse button at the **Paper Size** tab on the displayed dialogue box, shown below

- Click the down-arrow against the **Paper Size** box to reveal the list of available paper sizes

- Change the page size to your new choice, and press the **Default** button and confirm that you wish this change to affect all new documents based on the NORMAL template.

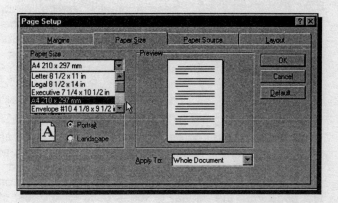

Check that the paper size matches that in your printer, otherwise you may get strange results. The orientation of the printed page is normally **Portrait** (text prints across the page width), but you could choose to change this to **Landscape** which prints across the page length, as long as your printer can print in landscape.

Modifying the Paper Source:

Clicking on the third Page Setup tab, displays yet another

dialogue box, part of which is shown here, from which you can select the paper source. You might have a printer that holds paper in trays, in which case you might want to specify that the first page (headed paper perhaps), should be taken from one tray, while the rest of the paper should be taken from a

different tray.

Modifying the Page Layout:

Clicking the last Page Setup tab displays the Layout dialogue box, part of which is shown here.

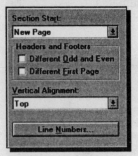 From this dialogue box you can set options for headers and footers, section breaks, vertical alignment and whether to add line numbers.

The default for **Section Start** is 'New Page' which allows the section to start at the top of the next page. Pressing the down arrow against this option, allows you to change this choice.

In the Headers and Footers box you can specify whether you want one header or footer for even- numbered pages and a different header or footer for odd-numbered pages. You can further specify if you want a different header or footer on the first page from the header or footer used for the rest of the document. Word can align the top line with the 'Top' margin, but this can be changed with the **Vertical Alignment** option.

Changing Other Default Options:

You can also change the default options available to you in Word for Windows, by selecting the **Tools, Options** command. Using the displayed Options dialogue box (shown on the next page) you can:

- Specify the default **View** options. For example, you can select whether non-printing characters, such as Tabs, Spaces, and Paragraph marks, are shown or not.

- Adjust the **General** Word settings, such as the colour of text and its background, and the units of measure.

- Adjust the **Print** settings, such as the **Reverse Print Order** mode, or choose to print the **Summary Info** or **Annotations**.

- Change the **Save** options, such as selecting the **Always Create Backup Copy** option for your work.

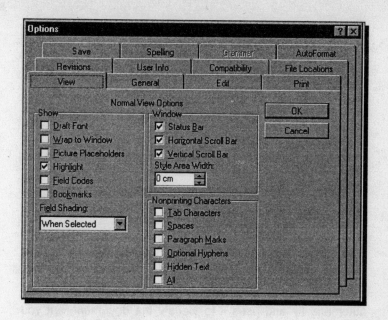

Saving to a File

To save a document to disc, use either of the following two commands:

- **File, Save** which is used when a document has previously been saved to disc in a named file; using this command automatically saves your work under the existing filename without prompting you.

- **File, Save As** command which is used when you want to save your document with a different name from the one you gave it already.

Using the **File, Save As** command (or the very first time you use the **File, Save** command when a document has no name), causes the dialogue box shown overleaf, to appear on your screen:

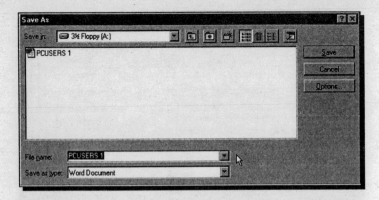

Note that the old document name (if it exists) is highlighted in the **File name** field box and the program is waiting for you to type a new name. Any name you type (don't use more than 255 characters) will replace the existing name. Filenames cannot include any of the following keyboard characters: /, \, >, <, *, ?, ", |, :, or ;. Word adds the file extension **.DOC** automatically and uses it to identify the document, but you don't see it.

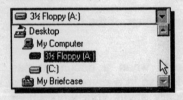

You can select a drive other than the one displayed, by clicking the down arrow against the **Save in** field. To save your work currently in memory, move the cursor into the **File name** box, and type **PCUSERS 1**.

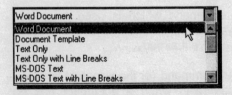

By clicking the **Save as type** button at the bottom of the Save As dialogue box, you can save the Document Template, or the Text Only parts of your work, or you can save your document in a variety of other formats, such as MS-DOS Text, Rich Text Format, or a number of WordPerfect formats.

Document Properties:

A useful feature in Word is the facility to add document properties to every file by selecting the **File, Properties** command.

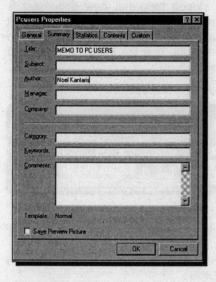

A Properties box, as shown here, opens for you to type additional information about your document.

In this box you can select to add a manager, company, or category name to group files together for ease of retrieval.

To do this on a more regular basis, make sure that the **Prompt for Document Properties** box in the Save Options dialogue box is selected and appears ticked.

Closing a Document:

There are several ways to close a document in Word. Once you have saved it you can click its 'x' close button, or double-click on the Document Control button at the left end of the menu bar; you would usually use these when you have several files open together.

If you want to close the current document, then open a new or another document, do the following:

- Choose **File, Close** to close the current document (remove it from your computer's memory) before using either

- **File, New** to create a new file, or

- **File, Open** to use an existing file.

If the document (or file) has changed since the last time it was saved, you will be given the option to save it before it is removed from memory.

If a document is not closed before a new document is opened, then both documents will be held in memory, but only one will be the current document. To find out which documents are held in memory, use the **Window** command to reveal the following menu:

In this case, the first document in the list is the current document, and to make another document the current one, either type the document number, or point at its name and click the left mouse button.

To close a document which is not the current document, use the **Window** command, make it current, and close it with one of the above methods.

4. EDITING WORD DOCUMENTS

It will not be long, when using Word, before you will need to edit your document. One of the first things you will notice is that misspelled words are unobtrusively underlined in a red wavy line, as shown here, and that the Tip Wizard advises you to right-click these words to correct them. This is possibly the most time-saving enhancement in the spell checker (to be discussed later).

Other editing could include deleting unwanted words or adding extra text in the document. All these operations are very easy to carry out.

For small deletions, such as letters or words, the easiest method to adopt is the use of the <Del> or <BkSp> keys. With the <Del> key, position the cursor on the left of the first letter you want to delete and press <Del>; the letter is deleted and the following text moves one space to the left. With the <BkSp> key, position the cursor immediately to the right of the character to be deleted and press <BkSp>; the cursor moves one space to the left pulling the rest of the line with it and overwriting the character to be deleted.

Word processing is usually carried out in the insert mode. Any characters typed will be inserted at the cursor location (insertion point) and the following text will be pushed to the right, and down, to make room. To insert blank lines in your text, place the cursor at the beginning of the line where the blank line is needed and press <Enter>. To remove the blank line, position the cursor on it and press <Del>.

When larger scale editing is needed you have several alternatives. You could first 'select' the text to be altered, then use the **Cut, Copy** and **Paste** operations available in the **Edit** sub-menu, or click on Toolbar button alternatives. Another method is to use the 'drag and drop' facility for copying or moving text.

Selecting Text

The procedure in Word, as with most Windows based applications, is first to select the text to be altered before any operation, such as formatting or editing, can be carried out on it. Selected text is highlighted on the screen. This can be carried out in two main ways:

A. Using the keyboard, to select:

- A block of text.

  Position the cursor on the first character of the block and hold down the <Shift> key while using the arrow keys to highlight the required text, then release the <Shift> key.

- A word.

  Use <Shift+End>.

- From the present cursor position to the beginning of the line.

  Use <Shift+Home>.

- From the present cursor position to the end of the document.

  Use <Shift+Ctrl+End>.

- From the present cursor position to the beginning of the document.

  Use <Shift+Ctrl+Home>.

B. With the mouse, to select:

- A block of text.

  Press the left mouse button at the beginning of the block and while holding it pressed, drag the cursor across the block so that the desired text is highlighted, then release the mouse button.

• A word.	Double-click within the word.
• A line.	Place the mouse pointer on the selection bar, just to the left of the line, and click once (for multiple lines, after selecting the first line, drag the pointer in the selection bar).
• A sentence.	Hold the <Ctrl> key down and click in the sentence.
• A paragraph.	Place the mouse pointer in the selection bar and double-click (for multiple paragraphs, after selecting the first paragraph, drag the pointer in the selection bar).
• The whole document.	Place the mouse pointer in the selection bar, hold the <Ctrl> key down and click once.

Copying Blocks of Text

Once text has been selected it can be copied to another location in your present document, to another Word document, or to another Windows application, via the clipboard. As with most of the editing and formatting operations there are several alternative ways of doing this, as follows:

- Use the **Edit, Copy** command sequence from the menu, to copy the selected text to the Windows clipboard, moving the cursor to the start of where you want the copied text to be placed, and using the **Edit, Paste** command.

- Use the quick key combinations, <Ctrl+Ins> (or <Ctrl+C>) to copy and <Shift+Ins> (or <Ctrl+V>) to paste, once the text to be copied has been selected, which does not require the menu bar to be activated.

- Use the 'Copy to clipboard' and 'Paste from clipboard' Toolbar buttons; you can of course only use this method with a mouse.

    To copy the same text again to another location, to any open window document or application, move the cursor to the new location and paste it there with any of these methods, as it is stored on the clipboard until it is replaced by the next Cut, or Copy operation.

- First select the text, then hold both the <Ctrl> and <Shift> keys depressed, place the cursor at the start of where you want the copied text to be and press the right mouse button. The new text will insert itself where placed, even if the overstrike mode is in operation. Text copied by this method is not placed on the clipboard, so multiple copies are not possible, as with the other methods.

Moving Blocks of Text

Selected text can be moved to any location in the same document by either of the following:

- Using the **Edit, Cut,** command or <Shift+Del> (or <Ctrl+X>).

- Clicking the 'Cut to clipboard' Toolbar button, shown here.

Next, move the cursor to the required new location and use either of the following procedures:

- The **Edit, Paste** command.

- Any other paste actions as described previously.

The moved text will be placed at the cursor location and will force any existing text to make room for it. This operation can be cancelled by simply pressing <Esc>. Once moved, multiple copies of the same text can be produced by other **Paste** operations.

Selected text can be moved by dragging the
mouse with the left button held down. The drag
pointer is an arrow with an attached square - the
vertical dotted line showing the point of insertion.

Deleting Blocks of Text

When text is 'cut' it is removed from the document, but
placed on the clipboard until further text is either copied or
cut. With Word any selected text can be deleted by pressing
Edit, Cut, or by pressing the <Del>, or <BkSp> keys.
However, using **Edit, Cut**, allows you to use the **Edit, Paste**
command, but using the <Del> or <BkSp> keys, does not.

The Undo Command

As text is lost with the delete command, you should use it
with caution, but if you do make a mistake all is not lost as
long as you act promptly. The **Edit, Undo** command or
<Ctrl+Z> (or <Alt+BkSp>) reverses your most recent editing
or formatting commands.

You can also use the Toolbar buttons, shown here, to

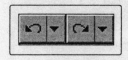

undo one of several editing or
formatting mistakes (press the down
arrow to the right of the left button to
see a list of your changes) or even
redo any one of the undo moves with

the right button.

Undo does not reverse any action once editing changes
have been saved to file. Only editing done since the last save
can be reversed.

Finding and Changing Text

Word allows you to search for specifically selected text, or
character combinations. To do this use:

- The **Find** or the **Replace** option from the **Edit**
  command sub-menu.

Using the **Find** option (<Ctrl+F>), will highlight each
occurrence of the supplied text in turn so that you can carry
out some action on it, such as change its font or appearance.

Using the **Replace** option (<Ctrl+H>), allows you to specify what replacement is to be automatically carried out. For example, in a long article you may decide to replace every occurrence of the word 'microcomputers' with the word 'PCs'.

To illustrate the **Replace** procedure, either select the option from the **Edit** sub-menu or use the quick key combination <Ctrl+H>. This opens the Replace dialogue box, displayed in the top half of the composite screen dump shown below.

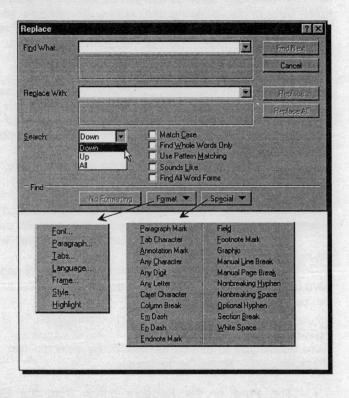

Towards the bottom of the dialogue box, there are five check boxes; the first two can be used to match the case of letters in the search string, and/or a whole word, while the last three can be used for pattern, 'sounds like' or 'word forms' matching.

The two buttons, **Format** and **Special**, situated at the bottom of the dialogue box, let you control how the search is carried out. The lists of available options, when either of these buttons is pressed, are displayed above. You will of course only see one or the other, but not both as shown here.

You can force both the search and the replace operations to work with exact text attributes. For example, selecting:

- The **Font** option from the list under **Format**, displays a dialogue box in which you select a font (such as Arial, Times New Roman, etc.); a font-style (such as regular, bold, italic, etc.); an underline option (such as single, double, etc.); and special effects (such as strike-through, superscript, subscript, etc.).

- The **Paragraph** option, lets you control indentation, spacing (before and after), and alignment.

- The **Style** option, allows you to search for, or replace, different paragraph styles. This can be useful if you develop a new style and want to change all the text of another style in a document to use your preferred style.

With the use of the **Special** button, you can search for, and replace, various specified document marks, tabs, hard returns, etc., or a combination of both these and text, as listed in the previous screen dump.

Advanced Search Operators:

The list below gives the key combinations of special characters to type into the **Find What** and **Replace With** boxes when the **Use Pattern Matching** box is checked.

Type	To find or replace
?	Any single character within a pattern. For example, searching for nec?, will find neck, connect, etc.
*	Any string of characters. For example, searching for c*r, will find such words as cellar, chillier, etc., also parts of words such

as <u>character</u>, and combinations of words such as <u>connect, cellar</u>.

[ ]	One of the specified characters. For example, searching for d[oi]g, will find such words as dog and dig.
[-]	Any single character in the specified range. For example, searching for [b-f]ore, will find such words as bore, core, fore, etc.
[!]	Any single character except the character inside the brackets. For example, searching for l[!o]ve, will find live, but not love.
[!s-z]	Any single character except characters in the range inside the brackets. For example, searching for [!s-z]ong, will find long but not song.
{n}	Exactly n occurrences of the previous character. For example, searching for me{2}t, will find meet but not met.
{n,}	At least n occurrences of the previous character. For example, searching for me{1,}t, will find met and meet.
{n,m}	From n to m occurrences of the previous character. For example, searching for 9{1,3}, will find 9, 99, and 999.
@	One or more occurrences of the previous character. For example, searching for ro@t, will find rot and root.
<	The beginning of a word. For example, searching for <on, will find on and onto, but not upon.
>	The end of a word. For example, searching for >on, will find on and upon, but not onto.

48

Page Breaks

The program automatically inserts a 'soft' page break in a document when a page of typed text is full. To force a manual, or hard page break, either type <Ctrl+Enter> or use the **Insert**, **Break** command and select **Page Break** in the dialogue box, as shown below.

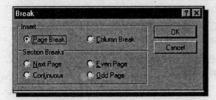

Pressing **OK** places a series of dots across the page to indicate the page break, as shown below. To delete manual page breaks place the cursor on the selection bar to the left of the page break mark, click once to highlight the line of dots, and press <Del>.

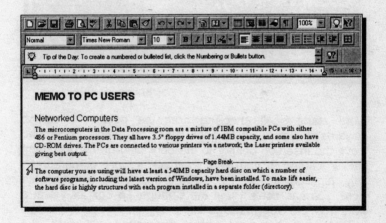

Soft page breaks which are automatically entered by the program at the end of pages, cannot be deleted.

Using the Spell Checker

The package has a very comprehensive spell checker which whenever it thinks it has found a misspelled word, underlines it with a red wavy line. To correct your document, right-click such words for alternatives.

However, the spell checker can also be used in another way. To spell check your document, either click the 'Spelling' button on the Standard Toolbar, shown here, or use the **Tools**, **Spelling** command (or **F7**) to open the dialogue box shown below (if necessary, use the **Tools, Language** command, select the correct dictionary and click the **Default** button).

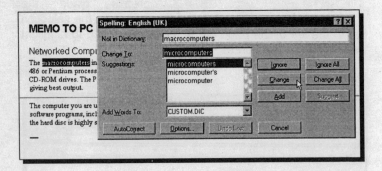

Word starts spell checking from the point of insertion onwards. If you want to spell check the whole document, move the insertion pointer to the beginning of the document before starting. If you want to check a word or paragraph only, highlight it first. Once Word has found a misspelled word, you can correct it in the **Change To** box, or select a word from the **Suggestions** list.

The main dictionary cannot be edited. However, the system has the ability to add specialised and personal dictionaries with the facility to customise and edit the latter. If you are using personal dictionaries and you use the spell checker and choose **Add**, the specified word is added to the dictionary.

Printing Documents

When Windows was first installed on your computer the printers you intend to use should have been selected, and the SETUP program should have installed the appropriate printer drivers. Before printing for the first time, you would be wise to ensure that your printer is in fact properly installed. To do this, click on **Start** then select **Settings** and click the **Printers** menu option to open the Printers dialogue box shown below.

Here, two printer drivers have been installed; an HP LaserJet 4M as the 'default' printer and an HP LaserJet 4/4M PostScript. In our case these are both configured to output to a printer via the parallel port LPT1. This refers to the socket at the back of your PC which is connected to your printer. LPT1 is short for Line Printer No. 1. Your selections may, obviously, not be the same.

To see how a printer is configured (whether to print to the parallel port or to a file), select it by clicking its icon, use the **File, Properties** command and click the Details tab of the displayed dialogue box.

Next, return to or reactivate Word and, if the document you

want to print is not in memory, either click the 'Open' button on the Toolbar, or use the **File, Open** command, to display the Open dialogue box shown on the next page.

Use the Open dialogue box to locate the file (document) you want to print, which will be found on the drive and folder (directory) on which you saved it originally. Select it and click the **Open** button (or double-click its name), to load it into your computer's memory.

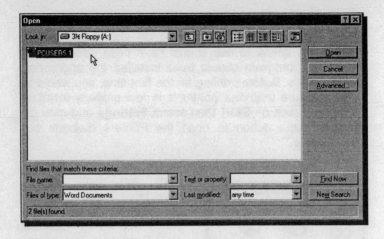

To print your document, do one of the following:

- Click the Print icon on the Toolbar, shown here, which prints the document using the current defaults.

- Use the **File, Print** command which opens the 'Print' box, shown below.

The settings in the Print dialogue box allow you to select the number of copies, and which pages, you want printed. You can also select to print the document, the summary information relating to that document, annotations, styles, etc., as shown in the drop-down list below.

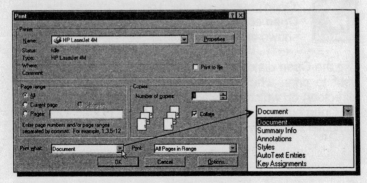

You can even change the selected printer by clicking the down arrow against the **Printer Name** box which displays the available printers on your system.

Clicking the **Properties** button on the Print dialogue box, displays the Properties dialogue box for the selected printer, shown below, which allows you to select the paper size, orientation needed, paper source, etc.

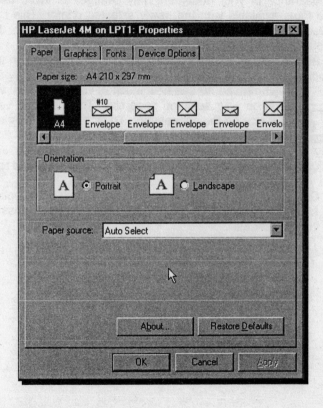

The **Options** button on the Print dialogue box, gives you access to some more advanced print options, such as printing in reverse order, with or without annotations, print hidden text or field codes, etc.

Clicking the **OK** button on these various multi-level dialogue boxes, causes Word to accept your selections and return you to the previous level dialogue box, until the Print dialogue box is reached. Selecting **OK** on this first level dialogue box, sends print output from Word to your selection, either the printer connected to your computer, or to an encoded file on disc. Selecting **Cancel** or **Close** on any level dialogue box, aborts the selections made at that level.

Do remember that, whenever you change printers, the appearance of your document may change, as Word uses the fonts available with the newly selected printer. This can affect the line lengths, which in turn will affect both the tabulation and pagination of your document.

Before printing to paper, click the Print Preview icon on the Toolbar, shown below, or use the **File, Print Preview** command, to see how much of your document will fit on your selected page size. This depends very 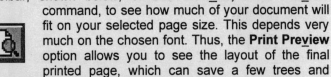 much on the chosen font. Thus, the **Print Preview** option allows you to see the layout of the final printed page, which can save a few trees and equally important to you, a lot of frustration and wear and tear on your printer.

Other enhancements of your document, such as selection of fonts, formatting of text, and pagination, will be discussed in the next chapter.

5. FORMATTING WORD DOCUMENTS

Formatting involves the appearance of individual words or even characters, the line spacing and alignment of paragraphs, and the overall page layout of the entire document. These functions are carried out in Word in several different ways.

Primary page layout is included in a document's Template and text formatting in a Template's styles. Within any document, however, you can override Paragraph Style formats by applying text formatting and enhancements manually to selected text. To immediately cancel manual formatting, select the text and use the

Edit, Undo

command, or (<Ctrl+Z>). The selected text reverts to its original format.

In the long term, you can cancel manual formatting by selecting the text and using the <Shift+Ctrl+N> key stroke. The text then reverts to its style format.

Formatting Text

If you use TrueType fonts, which are automatically installed when you set up Windows, Word uses the same font to display text on the screen and to print on paper. The screen fonts provide a very close approximation of printed characters. TrueType font names are preceded by ⊤ in the Font box on the Formatting toolbar and in the Font dialogue box which displays when you use the **Format, Font** command.

If you use non-TrueType fonts, then use a screen font that matches your printer font. If a matching font is not available, or if your printer driver does not provide screen font information, Windows chooses the screen font that most closely resembles the printer font.

Originally, the title of the memo **PCUSERS 1**, was typed in the 14 point size Arial typeface, while the subtitle and the main text were typed in 12 and 10 point size Arial, respectively.

To change this memo into what appears on the screen dump displayed below, first select the title of the memo and format it to bold, italics, 18 point size Arial and centre it between the margins, then select the subtitle and format it to bold, 14 point size Arial.

Finally select each paragraph of the main body of the memo in turn, and format it to 12 point size Times New Roman. All of this formatting can be achieved by using the buttons on the Formatting bar shown below (see also the section entitled 'Paragraph Alignment').

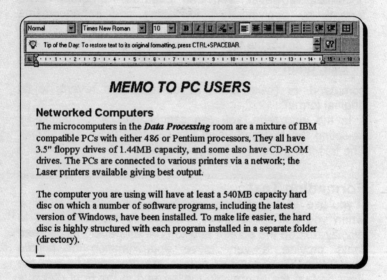

MEMO TO PC USERS

Networked Computers

The microcomputers in the *Data Processing* room are a mixture of IBM compatible PCs with either 486 or Pentium processors. They all have 3.5" floppy drives of 1.44MB capacity, and some also have CD-ROM drives. The PCs are connected to various printers via a network; the Laser printers available giving best output.

The computer you are using will have at least a 540MB capacity hard disc on which a number of software programs, including the latest version of Windows, have been installed. To make life easier, the hard disc is highly structured with each program installed in a separate folder (directory).

If you can't access these font styles, it will probably be because your printer does not support them, in which case you will need to select other fonts that are supported.

Save the result under the new filename **PCUSERS 2** - use the **File, Save As** command.

In Word all manual formatting, including the selection of font, point size, style (bold, italic, highlight, strike- through, hidden and capitals), colour, super/subscript, and various underlines, are carried out by first selecting the text and then executing the formatting command.

The easiest way of activating the formatting commands is from the Formatting toolbar. Another way is to use the

F̲ormat, **F̲ont**

command, which displays the following dialogue box:

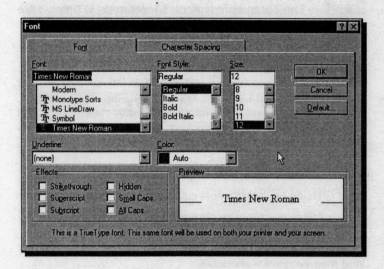

Yet another method is by using quick keys, some of which are listed below:

To Format	*Type*
Bold	Ctrl+B
Italic	Ctrl+I
Underline	Ctrl+U
Word underline	Ctrl+Shift+W
Double underline	Ctrl+Shift+D

There are quick keys to do almost anything, but the problem is remembering them! We find that those listed here are the most useful and the easiest to remember.

Text Enhancements

Word defines a paragraph, as any text which is followed by a paragraph mark, which is created by pressing the <Enter> key. So single line titles, as well as long typed text, can form paragraphs.

 The paragraph symbol, shown here, is only visible if you have selected it from the Toolbar.

Paragraph Alignment:

Word allows you to align a paragraph at the left margin (the default), at the right margin, centred between both margins, or justified between both margins. As with most operations there are several ways to perform alignment in Word. Three such methods are:

- Using buttons on the **Formatting bar**.

- Using keyboard short cuts, when available.

- Using the **Format**, **Paragraph** menu command.

The table below describes the buttons on the Formatting bar and their keystroke shortcuts.

Buttons on Formatting bar	Paragraph Alignment	Key-press Combination
	Left	<Ctrl+L>
	Centred	<Ctrl+E>
	Right	<Ctrl+R>
	Justified	<Ctrl+J>

The display below shows the dialogue box resulting from using the **Format**, **Paragraph** command in which you can specify any **Left, Right**, or **Special** indentation required.

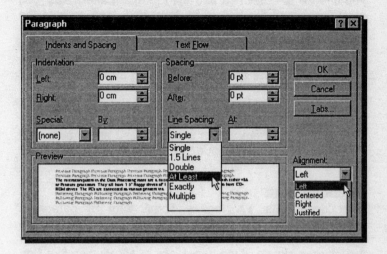

Paragraph Spacing:

The above Paragraph dialogue box can also be used to display a paragraph on screen, or print it on paper, in single-line, 1½-line, or double-line spacing. You can even set the spacing to any value you want by using the **At Least** option, as shown on the above screen dump, then specify what interval you want.

The available shortcut keys for paragraph spacing are as follows:

To Format	*Type*
Single-spaced lines	Ctrl+1
One-and-a-half-spaced lines	Ctrl+5
Double-spaced lines	Ctrl+2

Whichever of the above methods is used, formatting can take place either before or after the text is entered. If formatting is selected first, then text will type in the chosen format until a further formatting command is given. If, on the other hand, you choose to enter text and then format it afterwards, you must first select the text to be formatted, then activate the formatting.

Word gives you the choice of 4 units to work with, inches, centimetres, points or picas. These can be selected by using the **Tools**, **Options** command, choosing the **General** tab of

the displayed Options dialogue box, and clicking the down arrow against the **Measurement Units** list box, shown open here, which is to be found at the bottom of the dialogue box.

Indenting Text:

Most documents will require some form of paragraph indenting. An indent is the space between the margin and the edge of the text in the paragraph. When an indent is set (on the left or right side of the page), any justification on that side of the page sets at the indent, not the page border.

To illustrate indentation, open the file **PCUSERS 2**, select the first paragraph, and then choose the **Format**, **Paragraph** command. In the **Indentation** field, select 2.5cm for both **Left** and **Right**, as shown in the top half of the next page. On clicking **OK**, the first selected paragraph is displayed indented. Our screen dump shows the result of the indentation as well as the settings on the Paragraph dialogue box which caused it.

The **Indentation** option in the Paragraph dialogue box, can be used to create 'hanging' indents, where all the lines in a paragraph, including any text on the first line that follows a tab, are indented by a specified amount. This is often used in lists to emphasise certain points.

To illustrate the method, use the **PCUSERS 1** file and add at the end of it the text shown in the screen dump in the lower half of the next page.

MEMO TO PC USERS

Networked Computers

The microcomputers in the *Data Processing* room
eithe
3.5"
some
conn
Lase

The computer yo
disc on which a n
version of Windo
disc is highly stru
(directory).

In Windows 95 you can work with files in three different ways:

Name Description

My Computer Use the My Computer utility which Microsoft have spent much time and effort making as intuitive as possible.

Explorer Use the Windows Explorer, a much improved version of the older File Manager.

MS-DOS Use an MS-DOS Prompt window if you prefer to and are an expert with the DOS commands.

After you have typed the text in, save the enlarged memo as **PCUSERS 3**, before going on with formatting the new information. This is done as a precaution in case anything goes wrong with the formatting - it is sometimes much easier to reload a saved file (using the **File, Open** command), than it is to try to unscramble a wrongly formatted document!

Next, highlight the last 4 paragraphs above, use the **F̲ormat**, **Paragraph** command, and select 'Hanging' under **S̲pecial** and 3 cm under **By̲**. On clicking the **OK** button, the text formats as shown, but it is still highlighted. To remove the highlighting, click the mouse button anywhere on the page. The second and following lines of the paragraphs selected, should be indented 3 cm from the left margin, as shown below.

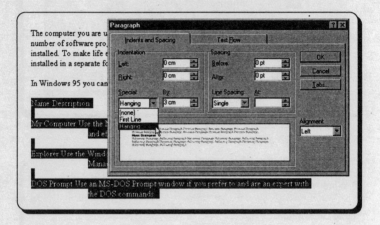

This is still not very inspiring, so to complete the effect we will edit the first lines of each paragraph as follows:

Place the cursor in front of the word 'Description' and press the <Tab> key once. This places the start of the word in the same column as the indented text of the other paragraphs. To complete the effect place tabs before the words 'Use' in the next three paragraphs, until your hanging indents are correct, as shown on the next page.

In Windows 95 you can work with files in three different ways:

Name	Description
My Computer	Use the My Computer utility which Microsoft have spent much time and effort making as intuitive as possible.
Explorer	Use the Windows Explorer, a much improved version of the older File Manager.
MS-DOS	Use an MS-DOS Prompt window if you prefer to and are an expert with the DOS commands.

This may seem like a complicated rigmarole to go through each time you want the hanging indent effect, but with Word you will eventually set up all your indents, etc., as styles in templates. Then all you do is click in a paragraph to produce them.

 When you finish formatting the document, save it under its current filename either with the **File, Save** command (<Ctrl+S>), or by clicking the Save button. This command does not display a dialogue box, so you use it when you do not need to make any changes to the saving operation.

Inserting Bullets:

Bullets are small characters you can insert, anywhere you like, in the text of your document to improve visual impact. In Word there are several choices for displaying lists with bullets or numbers. As well as the two Formatting bar buttons, others are made available through the

F<u>o</u>rmat, Bullets and <u>N</u>umbering

command, which displays the following dialogue box.

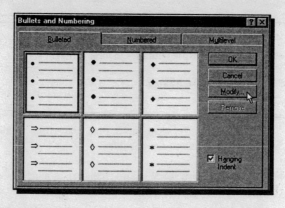

You can select any of the bullets shown here, or you could click the **Modify** button to change the size of the bullet, or the indentation. Further, by pressing the **Bullet** button on the Modify Bulleted List dialogue box which would be displayed, you could select any character from the Symbol typeface or other available type-faces.

If you select the **Numbered** or **Multilevel** tab, a similar dialogue box is displayed, giving you a choice of several numbering or multilevel systems. Once inserted, you can copy, move or cut a bulleted line in the same way as any other text. However, you can not delete a bullet with the <BkSp> or <Del> keys.

Inserting Date and Time:

You can insert today's date, the date the current document was created or was last revised, or a date or time that reflects the current system date and time into a document. Therefore, the date can be a date that changes, or a date that always stays the same. In either case, the date is inserted in a date field.

To insert a date field in your document, place the cursor where you want to insert the date, select the **Insert**, **Date and Time** command and choose one of the displayed date formats which suits you from the dialogue box shown on the next page.

Highlighting '30 March, 1996' (or whatever date is current), checking the **Update Automatically**, and pressing **OK**, inserts the date in our document at the chosen position.

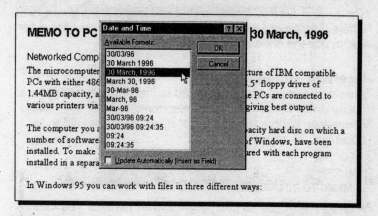

The above screen is a composite of the operation required and the result of that operation.

If you save a document with a date field in it and you open it a few days later, the date shown on it will be the original date the document was created. Should you want to update this date to the current date, right-click the field and select the **Update Field** option from the displayed Quick menu.

Word can either display the codes kept in a field, such as a date field, or the field results. To toggle between these two displays, place the insertion pointer anywhere within a field, click the right mouse button to display the Quick menu, shown below, and select the **Toggle Field Codes** option. The contents of the date field then changes to those shown below.

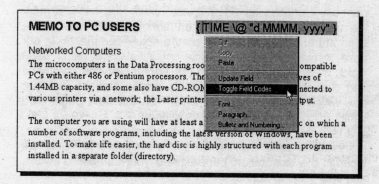

The reason for this facility is that you might want to mix two different types of formats, so the opportunity is presented for you to edit the code within a field.

Inserting Annotations:

Another powerful feature of Word is the facility to annotate a document. These act like electronic labels - initialled comments by the people who might have an input to a document, as shown below.

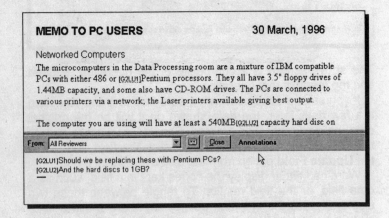

To add annotations to a document, place the cursor at the place you want to add a comment (or highlight a portion of text), and use the **Insert**, **Annotation** command.

Each person who views and edits the same document is normally identified as **A1**, **A2**, etc., which are used to mark the place in the text where an annotation is required. A separate annotation pane holds the actual comments. In our case instead of A1, etc., different initials are being used which were declared by using the **Tools**, **Options** command and clicking on the **User Info** tab on the Options dialogue box which displays what is shown on the next page. You could, of course use your initials instead.

It is in this dialogue box that you register your user name, initials to be used in the main text while your comments are typed in the 'annotation' pane against your numbered initials, and your mailing address.

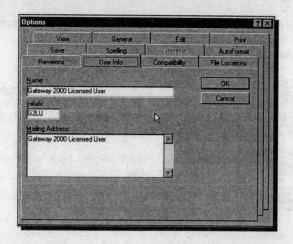

To open an annotation pane, when you need to read its contents, double-click on the numbered initials in the text with the mouse pointer. To remove an annotation, highlight the initials in the text and press <Del>.

Formatting with Page Tabs

You can format text in columns by using tab stops. Word has default left tab stops every 1.27 cm from the left margin, as shown here. This symbol appears on the left edge of the ruler below.

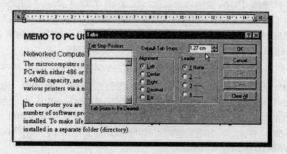

To set tabs, use either the **Format**, **Tabs** command which produces the Tab dialogue box, or click on the tab symbol on the left of the Ruler which cycles through the available tab stops.

The tab stop types available have the following function:

Button	Name	Effect
L	**Left**	Left aligns text after the tab stop.
⊥	**Centre**	Centres text on tab stop.
⌐	**Right**	Right aligns text after the tab stop.
⊥	**Decimal**	Aligns decimal point with tab stop.

To clear the ruler of tab settings press the **Clear All** button in the Tabs dialogue box. When you set a tab stop on the ruler, all default tab stops to the left of the one you are setting are removed. In addition, tab stops apply either to the paragraph containing the cursor, or to any selected paragraphs.

The easiest way to set a tab is to click on the tab type button you want and then point and click at the required position on the lower half of the ruler. To remove an added tab, point to it, click and drag it off the ruler.

If you want tabular text to be separated by characters instead of by spaces, select one of the three available characters from the **Leader** box in the Tabs dialogue box. The options are none (the default), dotted, dashed, or underline. The Contents and Index pages of this book are set with right tabs and dotted leader characters.

Note: As all paragraph formatting, such as tab stops, is placed at the end of a paragraph, if you want to carry the formatting of the current paragraph to the next, press <Enter>. If you don't want formatting to carry on, press the down arrow key instead.

Formatting with Styles

We saw earlier in Chapter 5, how you can format your work using Paragraph Styles, but we confined ourselves to using the default **Normal** style only. In this section we will get to grips with how to create, modify, use, and manage styles.

As mentioned previously, a Paragraph Style is a set of formatting instructions which you save so that you can use repeatedly within a document or in different documents. A collection of Paragraph Styles can be placed in a Template which could be appropriate for, say, all your memos, so it can be used to preserve uniformity. It maintains consistency and saves time by not having to format each paragraph individually.

Further, should you decide to change a style, all the paragraphs associated with that style reformat automatically. Finally, if you want to provide a pattern for shaping a final document, then you use what is known as a Template. All documents which have not been assigned a document template, use the **Normal.dot** global template, by default.

Paragraph Styles:

Paragraph Styles contain paragraph and character formats and a name can be attached to these formatting instructions. From then on, applying the style name is the same as formatting that paragraph with the same instructions.

You can create a style by example, either with the use of the Formatting bar or the keyboard, or you can create a style from scratch, before you use it, by selecting the **Format, Style** menu command. By far the simplest way of creating a style is by example.

Creating Paragraph Styles by Example: Previously, we spent some time manually creating some hanging indents in the last few paragraphs of the **PCUSERS 3** document. To create a style from this previous work, place the insertion pointer in one of these paragraphs, say, in the 'Name Description' line, and highlight the entire name of the existing style in the Formatting bar's Style box, as shown on the next page.

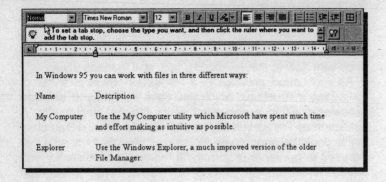

In Windows 95 you can work with files in three different ways:

Name	Description
My Computer	Use the My Computer utility which Microsoft have spent much time and effort making as intuitive as possible.
Explorer	Use the Windows Explorer, a much improved version of the older File Manager.

Then, type the new style name you want to create, say, 'Hanging Indent', and press <Enter>.

Finally, highlight the last three paragraphs with hanging indents and change their style to the new 'Hanging Indent', by clicking the mouse in the Style box button and selecting the appropriate style from the displayed list, as shown below. Save the result as **PCUSERS 4.**

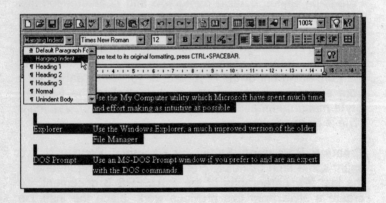

Creating Styles with the Menu Command: You can create, or change, a style before you apply any formatting to a paragraph, by using the **Format**, **Style** command. This displays the Style dialogue box, in which you can choose which style you want to change from the displayed **Styles** list.

Having selected the style you want to change (or not, as the case may be), click the **Modify** button which produces the Modify Style dialogue box. From here you can create a new style, or modify an existing style, by changing the formatting of characters, borders, paragraphs, and tab stops. You can even select which style should follow your current style.

Document Templates

A document template provides the overall pattern of your final document. It can contain:

- Styles to control your paragraph and formats.

- Page set-up options.

- Boilerplate text, which is text that remains the same in every document.

- AutoText (Glossary in previous versions), which is standard text and graphics that you could insert in a document by typing the name of the AutoText entry.

- Macros, which are programs that can change the menus and key assignments to comply with the type of document you are creating.

- Customised shortcuts, toolbars and menus.

If you don't assign a template to a document, then the default **Normal.dot** template is used by Word. To create a new document template, you either modify an existing one, create one from scratch, or create one based on the formatting of an existing document.

Creating a Document Template:

To illustrate the last point, we will create a simple document template, which we will call **PCuser**, based on the formatting of the **PCUSERS 4** document. But first, make sure you have defined the 'Hanging Indent' style as explained earlier.

To create a template based on an existing document:

- Open the existing document.

- Select the **File, Save As** command which displays the Save As dialogue box, shown below.

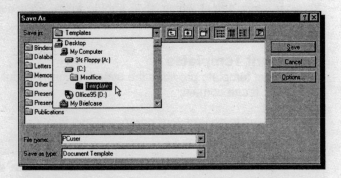

- In the **Save as type** box, select Document Template.

- In the **Save in** box, use the Templates folder which is in the Msoffice folder, which should have opened for you.

- In the **File name** box, type the name of the new template (PCuser in our example).

- Press the **Save** button, which opens the template file **PCuser.dot** in the Word working area.

- Add the text and graphics you want to appear in all new documents that you base on this template, and *delete* any items (including text) you do not want to appear (In our example, we deleted everything in the document, bar the heading).

- Click the Save icon on the Toolbar, and close the document.

To use the new template, do the following:

- Use the **File**, **New** command which causes the New dialogue box to be displayed, as shown below.

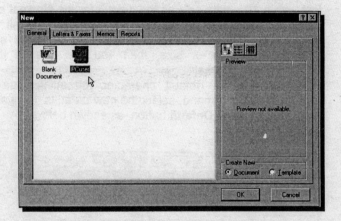

- Click the General tab and select the name of the template you want to use from the displayed list.

- Make sure that the radio button **Document** is selected, and click the **OK** button.

The new document will be using the selected template.

Templates can also contain Macros as well as AutoText; macros allow you to automate Word keystroke actions only, while AutoText speeds up the addition of boilerplate text and graphics into your document. However, the design of these features is beyond the scope of this book.

On the other hand, Word has a series of built-in templates to suit every occasion. These can be found, as seen in the above dialogue box, under the tabs of Letters & Faxes, Memos, and Reports. Try them.

Special Formatting Features

Word has several special formatting features which force text to override style and style sheet formatting. In what follows, we discuss the most important amongst these.

Changing the Default Character Format:

As we have seen, Word uses the Times New Roman type font with a 10 points size as the default for the **Normal** style, which is contained in the **Normal** template, for all new documents. If the majority of your work demands some different font style or size, then you can change these defaults to suit yourself.

To change the default character formatting, use the **Format**, **Font** command, select the new defaults you want to use, and press the **Default** button, as shown below:

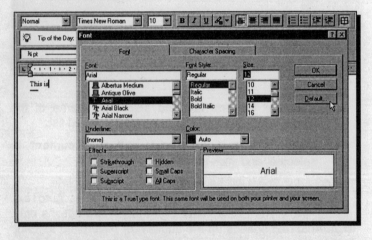

On pressing the **Default** button, the following dialogue box is displayed:

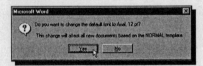

Pressing the **Yes** button, changes the default character settings for this and all subsequent new documents, but does not change already existing ones.

Inserting Special Characters and Symbols:

Word has a collection of Symbol fonts, such as the characters produced by the Symbol, Wingdings and Zapf Dingbats character sets, from which you can select characters and insert them into your document using the **Insert, Symbol** command.

When this command is executed, Word displays the following dialogue box:

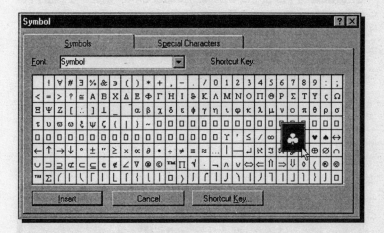

Pressing the down-arrow button next to the **Font** box, reveals the other available character sets. The set showing above is the Symbol set. If you point and click the left mouse button at a character within the set, it selects it. If you press down the left mouse button it magnifies the selected character, and if you double-click the left mouse button, it transfers the selected character to your document at the insertion point. A Symbol character can only be deleted with the <Del> key; you can not use the <BkSp> key to delete it.

The advantage of using Symbol is that Word embeds codes in your document which prevent you from changing the character by selecting it and changing to a different font. Thus, this type of formatting overrides any changes you might introduce with a new paragraph formatting.

Inserting Other Special Characters:

You can include other special characters in a document, such as optional hyphens, which remain invisible until they are needed to hyphenate a word at the end of a line; non-breaking hyphens, which prevent unwanted hyphenation; non-breaking spaces, which prevent two words from splitting at the end of a line; or opening and closing single quotes. To insert these characters, click at the **Special Characters** tab of the Symbol dialogue box which reveals the following:

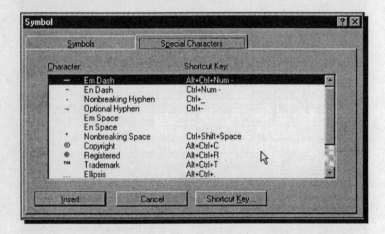

To insert one of these special characters, simply highlight the one required and press the **Insert** button. Using the **Shortcut Key** button displays the shortcut key combination attached to a symbol or special character, if it exists. You can also use this option to attach your preferred shortcut key combination to a symbol or special character.

6. FRAMES AND DRAWINGS

A frame in Word is like a 'mini-document' within the main document that allows you to create multiple layouts on the same page. A frame can contain text, a drawing, a picture, or an object such as a Lotus 1-2-3 worksheet, an AmiPro document, or a Word equation. A frame is not affected by the formatting of the main document. You can make document text wrap around, or flow above and below a frame; using the latter, you can create a heading to span a multi-column page. A page can contain multiple frames which can overlap.

Creating Frames

With Word you can create an empty frame by using the **Insert, Frame** command. You must, however, make sure that you are in Page Layout mode first. If you are not, the program will warn you and switch you to the required view.

Selecting this command, opens a cross-hair on your display and by moving this to the desired position, then pressing the left mouse button and dragging the mouse, you can insert a frame of the required size in your document, as shown below:

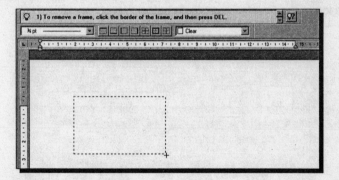

When you create a frame, it is placed in your document with the insertion point blinking in the upper left corner within the frame. When you type text, it wraps to fit the frame, but the frame expands vertically to accommodate all the typed text.

Moving Frames

A frame can be moved around your document by first selecting it, then dragging it with the mouse (move the mouse pointer over the frame until it turns to a four-headed arrow, as shown below in the top-left position, then click and drag to the desired position). The dotted outline shows the position in which the frame will be placed once you let go the left mouse button.

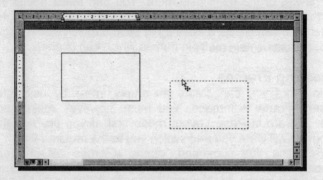

Another way of moving a frame is by using the **Format, Frame** command, and specifying its exact position on the page in the Frame box shown below.

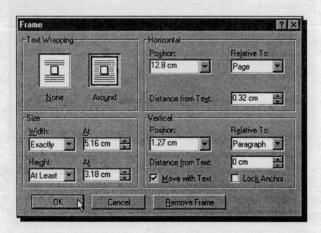

If a frame is placed in the middle of an existing paragraph (format the text into two columns (see page 104), before inserting the frame), the text of that paragraph can either wrap around the frame, as shown below, or be split above and below the frame. This depends on the selected **Text Wrapping** option in the Frame dialogue box, with **Around** being the default. Also by default, framed objects move with their surrounding text. To fix a frame at a specific position on a page, use the **Format, Frame** command and de-select the **Move with Text** option.

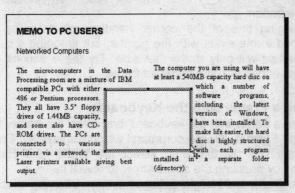

Word allows you to select a paragraph, a table or a drawing and then frame it, as shown below by using the **Insert, Frame** command.

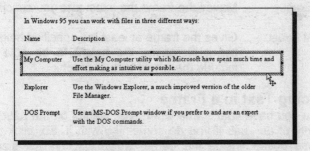

Once an object is framed, it can be moved in exactly the same way as an empty frame. To remove a frame, use the **Format, Frame** command and click the **Remove Frame** button.

Sizing Frames

There are two ways of sizing frames; with the mouse or the keyboard using the Frame dialogue box.

Sizing a Frame with the Mouse:

To size a frame with the mouse, select it so that the black selection handles appear around the frame, then move the mouse pointer over one of the selection handles until it turns to the two-headed sizing arrow. Drag the sizing arrow to change the frame to the required size, then release the mouse button.

Dragging one of the corner handles will drag the two attached frame sides with the pointer, but dragging a centre line handle will only move that side. Try these actions until you are happy with the resultant frame.

Sizing a Frame with the Keyboard:

To size a frame with the keyboard, first select the frame, then use the **Format, Frame** command which displays the Frame dialogue box. In this box, select the **Width** and **Height** options by pressing the down-arrow to reveal them.

The **Width** and **Height** options have the following effect:

Auto — Gives the frame the same size as the framed object.

Exactly — Makes the frame the exact size you specify.

At Least — Gives the frame at least the specified height, but it increases the height to be able to include the whole text, or graphic.

Placing Text in a Frame

Once you have your frame where you want it on the page, it is only of any use if you do something with it. So, click the mouse pointer inside the frame, which displays the sizing handles and places the cursor inside the frame, and type in some text (see screen display on next page). In our example, we also chose to name the style within the frame as 'framed' using the **Format, Style** command.

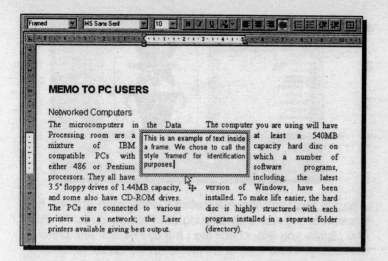

MEMO TO PC USERS

Networked Computers

The microcomputers in the Data Processing room are a mixture of IBM compatible PCs with either 486 or Pentium processors. They all have 3.5" floppy drives of 1.44MB capacity, and some also have CD-ROM drives. The PCs are connected to various printers via a network; the Laser printers available giving best output.

This is an example of text inside a frame. We chose to call the style 'framed' for identification purposes.

The computer you are using will have at least a 540MB capacity hard disc on which a number of software programs, including the latest version of Windows, have been installed. To make life easier, the hard disc is highly structured with each program installed in a separate folder (directory).

Next, and while the cursor is within the frame, select 'hanging indent' as the new style for the text inside your frame. The frame disappears, but the text remains as a redefined paragraph. If you choose the 'framed' style, the frame will reappear with the text intact inside it.

Now save this as **PCUSERS 5**, then click the mouse button outside the frame. This will cancel the frame selection and you will not be able to access, or edit, the text inside the frame until you next click inside it. Moving the mouse pointer over the frame area, turns it into a four-headed arrow, allowing you to move the frame to a new position when you click and drag. You can select the frame by single clicking which will let you re-size it; clicking once more anywhere on the text within the frame, allows you to edit that text.

Importing a Picture into a Frame

Create another frame on your page and click inside to select it. To import a picture into this frame, select the **Insert, Picture** command, which will open the dialogue box shown on the next page. This box allows you to enter the details of the picture, or graphic, that you want to import. The **List Files of Type** box gives you the choice of a wide range of graphic formats, but we will use a graphics sample from the **Msoffice\Clipart** folder.

The file selected above is called **Flower.bmp** and we have chosen to preview it by clicking the Preview button. If this is the picture you like, check the **Link to File** box and press the **OK** button. Word inserts the picture at the cursor position.

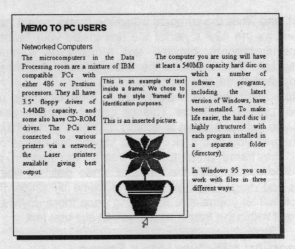

Save the resultant document as **PCUSERS 6**.

You can change the scaling factor of a picture and size it either by using the mouse, or by selecting it and using the **Format**, **Picture** command. The latter method causes the Picture dialogue box to be displayed, as shown on the next page.

If you want more white space around a picture, use negative numbers in the **Crop From** fields.

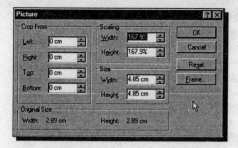

A picture can be inserted directly into your document at the cursor position, or you can first insert a frame, then insert the picture into the frame.

The advantage of the latter is that your text can be made to wrap around a frame, so you have more control over the inserted picture.

You can add a variety of borders to a frame, or a picture, by using the **Format**, **Borders and Shading** command which displays the following dialogue box:

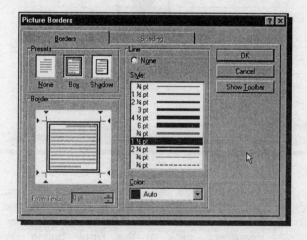

From here, you can select the thickness of the border line, whether it will have a single or double-line border, and whether the border should have a shadow or not.

For frames containing text, you can also choose the type of shading you prefer within the border area by selecting the frame, then using the **Format**, **Borders and Shading** command, and clicking the **Shading** tab. This facility is not available to a frame containing a picture.

The Drawing Tool

As long as you have a mouse, you can use Word's Draw tool to create, or edit, a picture consisting of lines, arcs, ellipses, rectangles, and even text boxes. These can either exist in their own right, or be additions to a picture.

If you want to add a drawing to an existing picture, either double-click it, or select it and use the **Edit, Picture Object** command. Activating this command while the picture of the flowerpot in **PCUSERS 6** document is selected, produces the following display:

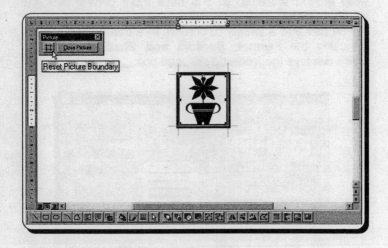

The Draw tool cannot be activated with either of the above methods if you are dealing with a frame that contains text.

To add a drawing to any frame or to any other part of your document, click at the Draw button on the Standard Toolbar, shown here. To actually draw within a frame you must first select it before starting to draw.

Whichever way you activate the Draw tool, Word displays a new set of icons at the bottom of the screen, as shown above. These can be moved to any part of the screen by dragging them to the new position. You could even form a third Toolbar at the top of the screen.

The Drawing icons allow you to carry out the following tasks:

Drawing ☒

Draw a line	Draw a rectangle
Draw an ellipse	Draw an arc
Draw in freeform	Text Box
Callout	Format Callout
Fill Colour	Line Colour
Line Style	Select Draw Objects
Bring to Front	Send to Back
Bring to Front of Text	Send Behind Text
Group	Ungroup
Flip Horizontal	Flip Vertical
Rotate Right	Reshape
Snap to Grid	Align Drawing Objects
Create Picture	Insert Frame

The effects of these drawing tools can be superimposed on either the document area or within a frame which might contain a picture. The result is that you can annotate drawings and pictures to your total satisfaction.

Creating a Drawing

To create an object, click on the required Draw button, such as the ellipse or rectangle, position the mouse pointer where you want to create the object on the screen, and then drag the mouse to draw the object. Hold the <Shift> key while you drag the mouse to create a perfect circle or square. If you do not hold <Shift>, Word creates an ellipse or a rectangle.

You can use the Freehand/Polygon Draw button to create freehand objects. First click on the Freehand button, then position the mouse pointer where you want to create the object on the screen. If you then press the left mouse button and keep it pressed, you can draw freehand. If, on the other hand, you click the left mouse button, the edge of the line attaches itself on the drawing area, at the point of contact. A straight line can then be drawn between that point and the next point on which you happen to click the mouse button. In this way you can draw polygons. When you finish drawing with either of these two methods, either double-click or press the <Esc> key to finish.

Editing a Drawing:

To select an object, first click the 'Selection Arrow' button and then click the desired object. Word displays black handles around the object selected.

You can move an object, or multiple objects, within a draw area by selecting them and dragging to the desired position. To copy an object, click at the object, then use the **Edit, Copy** / **Edit, Paste** commands.

To size an object, position the mouse pointer on a black handle and then drag the handle until the object is the desired shape and size.

To delete an object, select the object and press <Del>. To delete a drawing, hold the <Shift> key down and click each object in turn that makes up the drawing, unless they are grouped or framed, then press <Del>.

Do try out some of these commands using the **PCUSERS 6** document file. You could experiment with different text fonts, and try to edit the cat picture. As long as you do not save the results of your experimentation under the same file name, you can try different variations to the layout without fear of losing the contents of the original file.

Using Layered Drawings:

You can use Draw's Bring to Front or Send to Back buttons to determine the order of layered drawings. Drawings, or pictures, layered on top of each other can create useful visual effects, provided you remember that the top drawing and/or picture obscures the one below it, as shown below.

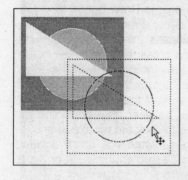

Here we have used Draw's Rectangle, Ellipse, and Freeform buttons to draw the three displayed shapes. The order you draw these is not important as you can use the Bring to Front and Send to Back buttons to rearrange them to your taste. We then selected each shape in turn, and used the Fill Colour button to give them different shades. Finally, we selected each shape, while holding down the <Shift> key, then used the Group button to lock them together, before attempting to move the whole group down and to the right (you can tell they are grouped because attempting to move them, moves the whole group, shown above in a dotted outline).

Changing Draw's Defaults

You can change the **Fill** colour palette, **Line** thickness, colour and arrowhead style, and **Size and Position** of your

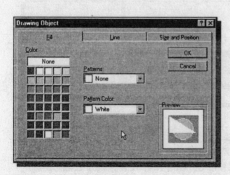

drawing by using the **Format, Drawing Object** command, which displays the Drawing Object dialogue box shown here. You can even preview proposed changes to the selected drawing before accepting them.

87

Inserting Objects into a Document

You can insert an Object into a document by using the **Insert, Object** command which causes the following dialogue box to appear on your screen:

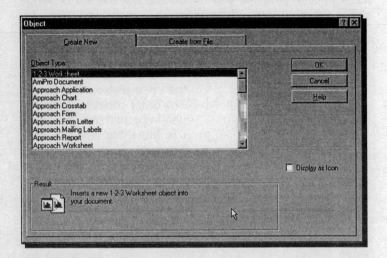

From here, you can choose different 'Object Types', from Lotus 1-2-3 Worksheets to Word Documents. For example, if you select 'Microsoft Equation 2' from the **Object Type** list, Word displays the Equation Editor shown below. If Word warns you that the Equation Editor requires the MT Extra (TrueType) font, follow the instructions on the next page.

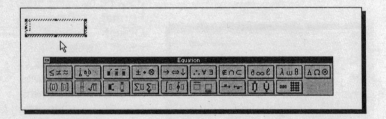

This allows you to build mathematical equations which can then be included in your Word for Windows document (see Appendix C for more details on this and a worked example).

Note: To install the MT Extra (TrueType) font, click the **Start** button on the Task bar and use the **Settings, Control Panel** command. In the displayed Control Panel window, double-click the Fonts icon and use the **File, Install New Font** command. Next, specify in the **Folders** field of the Add Fonts dialogue box the \windows\fonts folder. When all the fonts are listed, press the **Select All** button, followed by the **OK** button. From this point on, follow the instructions on the screen, remembering that already installed fonts, need not be re-installed.

If, on the other hand, you select Microsoft Graph 5.0, and you don't have a table in your document, the following screen is displayed:

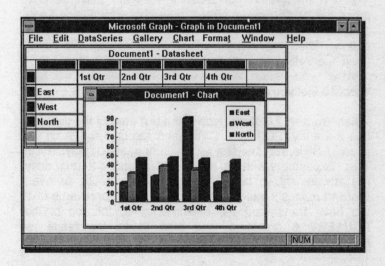

This is an internal Word example, showing the capabilities of the package. If you did have a table within your document which included information that could be graphed (see next chapter), and you had selected the area of the table you wanted to display as a graph, then Word would have displayed the contents of the selected portion of your table in an appropriate chart-type graph.

Finally, selecting Microsoft WordArt 2.0 causes the display shown below to appear on your screen. If Word informs you that it cannot find the Microsoft WordArt file, do the following:

Note: To install Microsoft WordArt 2.0, click the **Start** button on the Task bar and use the **Settings, Control Panel** command. In the displayed Control Panel window, double-click the **Add/Remove Programs** icon, and press the Install/Uninstall tap of the displayed dialogue box, followed by the **Install** button. The Run Installation Program will search for the SETUP program, first by accessing the A:\ drive, followed by any other installed drives. When the program is found, press the **Finish** button, which causes the Office Setup screen to be displayed.

In the Installation Maintenance Program dialogue box, press the **Add/Remove** button, then check the Office Tools entry in the **Options** list and press the **Change Options** button. When the various Office Tools options are listed, press the **Select All** button, followed by the **OK** button.

When you restart Windows, the new settings will take effect so that you can use WordArt 2.0.

When WordArt 2.0 starts, type in the text area of the dialogue box the entry 'PC Users Club', then selected the 'Arch Up (Curve)' Style from the first list which normally displays 'Plain Text'. Experiment with the new Toolbar buttons to reproduce the artwork shown below. As you will no doubt discover, WordArt makes it easy to slant, rotate, curve, or reverse text. We have transferred the above entry to the top of the **PCUSERS 6** document and then saved the result as **PCUSERS 7**.

7. MORE ADVANCED TECHNIQUES

Microsoft has built many advanced features into Word. Amongst these, we will examine here what you are most likely to need and in the order we assume you will require them. We shall examine document spell and grammar checking, the use of the thesaurus, page numbering, inclusion of headers/footers and footnotes.

Document Checking

When you have entered all the text and graphics into your document and selected suitable formats, there is only the process of correcting your work before printing the final copy. Word has many built-in tools to speed this process up and we will briefly describe the main ones here. There is also a set of Toolbar buttons for document checking and correcting.

Using the Spell Checker:

Most people have trouble spelling at least some words, but with Word that is not a problem. The package has a very comprehensive spell checker and has the ability to add specialised and personal dictionaries. The main dictionary contains more that 100,000 words which cannot be edited. The user dictionary you can customise and edit. If you are using personal dictionaries (see next page) and you use the spell checker and choose **Add**, Word adds the word to the specified user dictionary, which should have the file extension .dic.

To spell check your document, either click the 'Spelling' button on the Standard Toolbar, shown here, or use the **Tools**, **Spelling** command (or **F7**) to open the dialogue box shown on the next page.

Word starts spell checking from the point of insertion onwards. If you want to check a word or paragraph only, highlight it first. If you want to spell check the whole document, move the insertion point to the beginning of the document before starting. Once Word has found a misspelled word, you can correct it in the **Change To** box, or select a word from the **Suggestions** list.

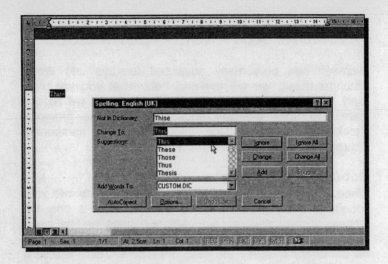

Word will produce a suggestions list only if the **Al̲ways Suggest** option from the Options dialogue box, shown below, is checked. This dialogue box is displayed if you press the **O̲ptions** button from the opening dialogue box.

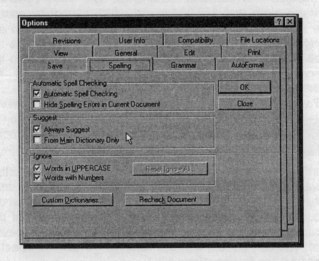

To use a personal dictionary, uncheck the **From Main Dictionary Only** box (if it is checked), and click the **Custom Dictionaries** button. This opens a further dialogue box, shown below.

To use a custom dictionary, check the box to the left of the dictionary name and press the **Add** button. The **New** button allows you to create a new custom dictionary which you will have to name and save before you can use it.

In the Options dialogue box you can select **Words in UPPERCASE** which will cause the spell checker to ignore words in all uppercase letters, and/or you can select **Words with Numbers** which forces the spell checker to ignore all words that include numbers.

When the correct word appears in the **Change To** box (you could choose a different word from the **Suggestions** list), select the **Change** button to replace the misspelled word in your document with the selected word. You select the **Change** button to correct only the current error, otherwise use the **Change All** button to change every future occurrence of the incorrect word in the document.

If you don't want to change the word in your document, use the **Ignore** button to leave that word as is, or the **Ignore All** button to ignore all future occurrences of the word in the document. If, on the other hand, Word comes across a specialised word that it thinks is misspelled, but it is not, you can add it to the customised dictionary named in the **Add Words To** box.

The customised dictionary is kept in the **Windows\Msapps\Proof** folder and can be opened like any other file, so that you can edit it. Words are kept in it in alphabetical order.

If you create a custom dictionary in a language other than English, select one from the **Language** list in the Custom Dictionaries dialogue box before pressing the **OK** button. To install the language dictionary, use the **Tools, Language** command to mark the text and identify the language it is written in, otherwise, Word will assume that the whole document is written in English. When this is done, Word will use the custom dictionary in the identified language to check text formatted in that language.

You can use the AutoCorrect feature to correct the spelling of words as you type. When this feature is activated and you make a mistake as you type, AutoCorrect replaces it with the correct word. This feature can also be used to replace certain key presses with specialised symbols, such as (C) with ©, and many more. To correct typing errors automatically, use the **Tools, AutoCorrect** command and select the **Replace Text as You Type** option in the displayed dialogue box, shown below.

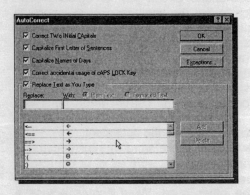

To add an AutoCorrect word while spell checking, click the **AutoCorrect** button in the Spelling dialogue box.

When Word finds double words, for example, yes yes, the **Not in Dictionary** box changes to the **Repeated Word** box with the repeated word displayed, and the **Change** button becomes a **Delete** button. If you want to delete one of the repeated words, leave the **Change To** box blank, and press the **Delete** button.

Using the Thesaurus:

If you are not sure of the meaning of a word, or you want to use an alternative word in your document, then the thesaurus is an indispensable tool. To use the thesaurus, simply place the cursor on the word you want to look up and select **Tools, Thesaurus** (or <Shift+F7>). As long as the word is recognised the following box will open.

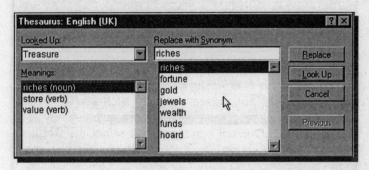

This is a very powerful tool. You can see information about an item in the **Meanings** list, or you can look up a synonym in the **Synonym** list. To change the word in the **Replace with Synonym** text box, select an offered word in either the **Meanings** or **Synonym** list box, or type a word directly into the text box.

You can use the thesaurus like a simple dictionary by typing any word into the **Replace with Synonym** box and selecting **Look Up**. If the word is recognised, lists of its meaning variations and synonyms will be displayed. Pressing the **Replace** button will place the word into the document.

The Grammar Checker:

The grammar checker provided with Word for Windows 95 is similar to that of Word 6, but you must first customise it to your requirements. This will be explained shortly with an example.

Note: Always save a document before using this facility because if a program error occurs, Word will be closed down and you will lose your work. In case of any such problems refer to the 'Warning' at the bottom of page 117.

To illustrate the use of the grammar checker, open the **PCUSERS 4** file and select the **Tools**, **Grammar** command. The grammar checker begins by highlighting the first sentence of the memo and displays the following screen:

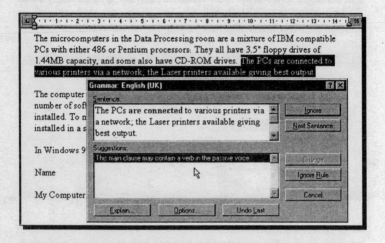

Note the contents of the **Suggestions** text box. This same message was also given for every sentence in the document. The message reads 'This main clause may contain a verb in the passive voice'. On pressing the **Explain** button, the following Grammar Explanation box is displayed:

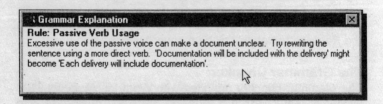

The analysis carried out previously was made with the **For Business Writing** option selected (see next page), which perhaps explains the comments of the grammar checker. When the option was changed to **For Casual Writing**, the same suggestions were made regarding the 'passive voice' with the same explanations.

With Word's grammar checker, you have the choice of three pre-set types of writing styles, namely 'Strictly (all rules)', 'For Business Writing', and 'For Casual Writing'. You also have the choice of three Custom styles. One of these can be selected by pressing the **Options** button of the Grammar dialogue box which displays the left dialogue box, shown in the composite below. Further, each of the selected styles can be customised by pressing the **Customize Settings** button which displays an additional dialogue box, also shown below.

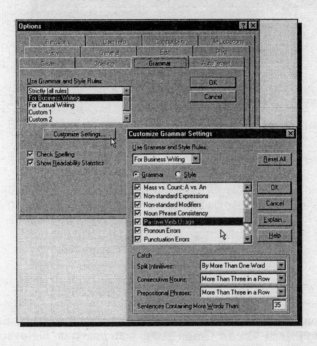

As you can see, you will need to spend quite some time customising the way the grammar checker works. Perhaps you might choose to stop it from re-checking your spelling by clicking at the **Check Spelling** box to be found at the bottom-left corner of the Options dialogue box.

You can also stop the grammar checker alerting you with reference to passive verbs, by simply de-selecting the option from the **Grammar** list box of the Customize Grammar Settings dialogue box.

97

If you persevere to the end of the document, Word displays the following Readability Statistics dialogue box:

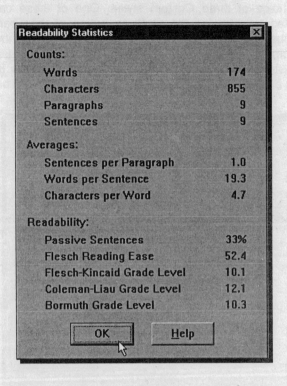

This gives a wealth of information, including readability measurements, under such terms as Flesch Reading Ease and Flesch-Kincaid Grade Level, both based on the average number of syllables per word and average number of words per sentence (the first giving scores between 0-100 with standard writing range from 60 to 70, while the second giving the grade-school level of understanding with standard writing scoring between 7 and 8).

The last two categories under the readability section measure word length in characters and sentence length in words to determine a grade level.

Document Enhancements

In this section we discuss features that enhance a document's appearance, such as page numbering, use of headers and footers, and use of footnotes.

Page Numbering:

If you need to number the pages of a document, but not the first page, use the **Insert, Page Numbers** command, which displays the following dialogue box:

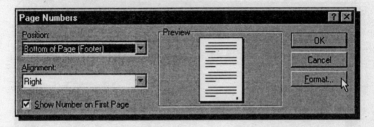

Use this box to specify the position of the page numbers in your document and their alignment. Selecting the **Format** button, opens another dialogue box, as shown below:

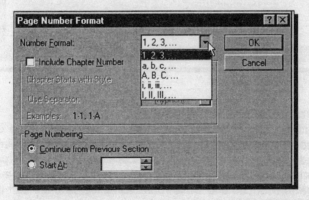

From this dialogue box you can select the **Number Format** from the following alternatives, '1, a, A, i, or I'; the more usual style being the first option, as used in this book. The 'Page Numbering' option gives you two alternatives; **Continue from Previous Section**, or **Start At** a specified number.

To illustrate page numbering open the **PCUSERS 7** document and use the **Insert, Page Numbers** command. Then, select 'Center' from the **Alignment** list box and make sure that the **Show Number on First Page** box is checked. Next, press the **Format** button, select **Start At 1** at the bottom of the second dialogue box, and press the **OK** button on each dialogue box. The result is a number '1' appearing centrally in a footer at the bottom of page 1, as shown below.

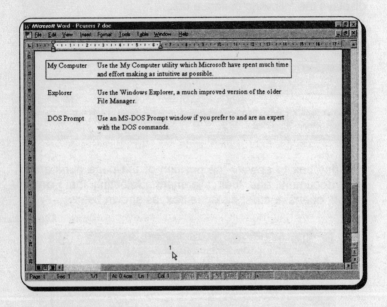

Using Headers and Footers:

Headers consist of text placed in the top margin area of a page, whereas footers are text in the bottom margin. Simple headers or footers in Word can consist of text and a page number, which are produced in the same position of every page in a document, while more complicated ones can also contain graphics images.

Word allows you to have one header/footer for the first page of a document, or section of a document, and a different one for the rest of the document. It also allows you to select a different header or footer for odd or even pages.

To insert a header or footer in a document, select the **View, Header and Footer** command, which causes Word to display the following:

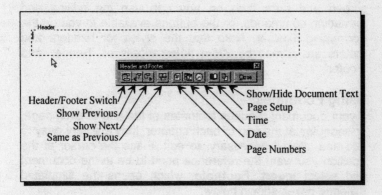

Header/Footer Switch
Show Previous
Show Next
Same as Previous
Show/Hide Document Text
Page Setup
Time
Date
Page Numbers

From here you can switch between header and footer by clicking the first button on the Header and Footer Bar. To adjust the horizontal position of a header or footer, use the 'Show Previous' and 'Show Next' buttons, or to adjust the vertical position of a header or footer use the 'Show Previous', 'Show Next' and 'Page Setup' buttons. These same three buttons can also be used to create a different header or footer for the first page of a document, or to create different headers and footers for odd and even pages.

In the example below, we chose to type 'Chapter 7' in the header panel, then we pressed <Tab> and typed 'Page' followed by a space, then pressed the 'Page Numbers' button on the Header and Footer Bar, which inserted the numeral 1, then we pressed <Tab> and pressed the time button.

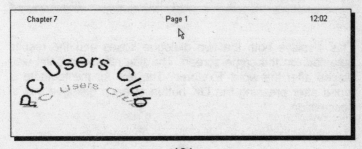

Chapter 7   Page 1   12:02

Once you select the **Close** button, headers and footers can be formatted and edited like any other text. To edit a header or footer, simply point to the appropriate panel and double-click. The Header and Footer Bar will appear on the screen and from then on you can use the editing and formatting commands, or the buttons available to you on the Formatting Toolbar. Note that the styles for headers and footers are named by Word automatically as 'Header' and 'Footer'.

Using Footnotes:

If your document requires footnotes at the end of each page, or endnotes at the end of each chapter, they are very easy to add and later, if necessary, to edit. Place the cursor at the position you want the reference point to be in the document and select **Insert, Footnote**, which opens the simulated dialogue boxes shown below:

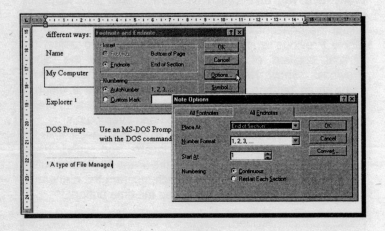

This displays both the two dialogue boxes and the results obtained, on the same screen. The first reference point was placed after the word 'Explorer'. The text for the footnote is typed after pressing the **OK** button of each dialogue box in succession.

The default option in the first dialogue box is **AutoNumber**. If you choose to press the **Options** button in this box, Word displays the second dialogue box which has two tabs. Selecting the **All** **F**ootnotes tab, allows you to choose where to place footnotes; 'Bottom of Page' or 'Beneath Text'. Selecting the **All** **E**ndnotes tab, allows you to place endnotes at the 'End of Section' or at the 'End of Document'. You could also choose from this second dialogue box the **Number Format**, the reference to **Start** **A**t a specific number or character, and the **Numbering** style.

If you wanted to type a reference mark of your own choosing, then select the **Custom Mark** from the first dialogue box. Pressing the **Symbol** button allows you the use of endless characters, particularly if you choose the 'Symbol' or 'Wingdings' styles in the **Symbols from** list, as shown below.

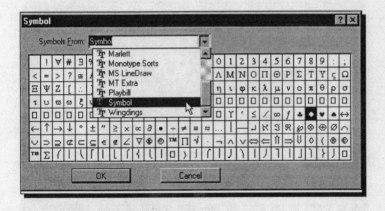

Once you have decided on your selection, save the resultant work under the filename **PCUSERS 8**.

Using Multiple Columns on a Page:

You can quickly modify the number of displayed columns, either for the whole document or for selected text by using the Columns button from the Toolbar, shown here. However, if you want more control over how the columns are displayed, then use the **Format, Columns** command. Below, we have selected the second paragraph of the **PCUSERS 8** memo and then used the **Format, Columns** command to format it in two columns with 1.27cm in between the two columns.

To see how the 'Preview' page changes, click the appropriate button on the **Presets** field of the Columns dialogue box. Now change the **Spacing** (otherwise known as gutter width) to see how to set the separation zones between columns.

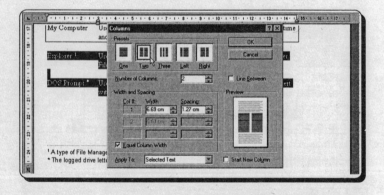

If you want to be able to see the result of your selection on your actual text, use the **View** command and select the **Page Layout** mode. As usual, you will only see your selected text in two columns, after you press the **OK** button on the Columns dialogue box.

8. USING TABLES AND GRAPHS

The ability to use 'Tables' is built into most top-range word processors these days. At first glance the process might look complicated and perhaps only a small percentage of users take advantage of the facility, which is a pity because using a 'Table' has many possibilities. If you have worked with a spreadsheet, such as Excel or Lotus 1-2-3, then you are familiar with tables.

Tables are used to create adjacent columns of text and numeric data. A table is simply a grid of columns and rows with the intersection of a column and row forming a rectangular box which is referred to as a 'cell'. In Word you can include pictures, charts, notes, footnotes, tabs, and page breaks in your tables. There are several ways to place information into a table:

- Type the desired text, or numeric data.
- Paste text from the main document.
- Link two tables within a document.
- Insert data created in another application.
- Import a picture.
- Create a chart on information held in a table.

The data is placed into individual cells that are organised into columns and rows, similar to a spreadsheet. You can modify the appearance of table data by applying text formatting and enhancements, or by using different paragraph styles.

Creating a Table

Tables can be created either by pressing the 'Table' button on the toolbar, shown here, or by using the **Table, Insert Table** command. Using the latter, displays the dialogue box shown on the next page, which enables you to size the column widths at that point.

As an example we will step through the process of creating the table shown on the next page. Open the **PCUSERS 8** file, place the insertion point at the end of the file (or where you want the table), then click on the 'Table' button and drag down and to the right.

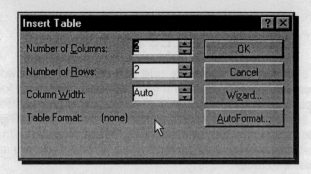

As you drag the mouse, the 'Table' button expands to create the grid of rows and columns. At the bottom of the box there is an automatic display of the number of rows and columns you are selecting by this method. When you release the mouse button, a table is inserted in your document the size of the selected grid.

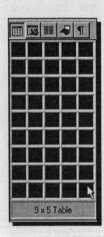

For our example, we require a 9 x 5 cell table. Once this appears in position, the cursor is placed in the top left cell awaiting your input. The cells forming the table, are displayed with dotted lines around each cell, if the **Table, Gridlines** menu option is checked.

To move around in a table, simply click the desired cell, or use one of the keyboard commands listed below.

Navigating with the Keyboard :

To navigate around a table when using the keyboard, use the following keys:

Press this	*To do this*
Tab	Moves the insertion point right one cell, in the same row, and from the last cell in one row to the first cell in the next row. If the cell contains information it highlights the contents.

Shift+Tab	Moves the insertion point left one cell. If the cell contains information it highlights the contents.
↑,↓,←, and →	Moves the insertion point within cells, between cells, and between the cells in a table and the main document text.
Home	Moves the insertion point to the beginning of the current line within a cell.
Alt+Home	Moves the insertion point to the first column in the current row.
End	Moves the insertion point to the end of the current line within a cell.
Alt+End	Moves the insertion point to the last column in the current row.
Alt+PgUp	Moves the insertion point to the top cell in the column.
Alt+PgDn	Moves the insertion point to the bottom cell in the column.

Now type in the information below and format your table using either the **Format, Paragraph** command or the buttons on the Formatting Toolbar to align the contents of the various columns as shown. The heading does not form part of the table. To change column width or row height, see next page.

Types of Removable Discs

Description	Capacity Kbytes	Price/Unit Pence	Number Bought	Cost in £
Double-sided floppies	360	40	20	
High-density floppies	1,200	60	40	
Double-sided stiffies	720	80	60	
High-density stiffies	1,440	100	80	
Removable hard discs	105,000	6500	1	
			Total	

Changing Column Width and Row Height:

The column width of selected cells or entire columns can be changed by dragging the table column markers on the ruler or by dragging the column boundaries, as shown in the adjacent display.

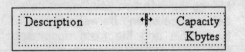

You can also drag a column boundary while holding down other keys. The overall effects of these actions is as follows:

Keys	*Effect*
No key	all columns to the right are re-sized proportionally with the overall width of the table remaining the same size.
Shift key	only the column to the right is re-sized with the overall width of the table remaining the same.
Ctrl key	all columns to the right become the same size which changes the overall width of the table.
Shift+Ctrl keys	all columns to the right retain their size which changes the overall width of the table.

The height of a row depends on its contents. As you type text into a cell, its height increases to accommodate it. You can also insert empty lines before or after the text by pressing the <Enter> key, which also increases the height of a cell. All other cells in that row become the same height as the largest cell.

The width of a column and the height of a row can also be changed by using the **Table, Cell Height and Width** command.

When you have finished, save your work under the filename **PCUSERS 9**. We will use this table to show you how you can insert expressions into cells to make your table behave just like a spreadsheet.

Entering Expressions:

To enter an expression into a table's cell, so that you can carry out spreadsheet type calculations, highlight the cell and use the **Table, Formula** command which displays the following dialogue box:

Types of Removable Discs

Description	Capacity Kbytes	Price/Unit Pence	Number Bought	Cost in £
Double-sided floppies	360	40	20	
High-density floppies	1,200	60	40	
Double-sided stiffies	720	80	60	
High-density stiffies	1,440	100	80	
Removable hard discs	105,000	6500	1	

Formula

Formula:
=SUM(LEFT)

Number Format:

Paste Function: Paste Bookmark:

OK   Cancel

Word analyses the table and suggests an appropriate formula in the **Formula** box. In the above situation, it has found numbers in cells to the left of the highlighted cell, therefore it suggests the SUM(LEFT) formula. To replace this formula with another formula, simply delete it from the **Formula** box and type the new formula preceded by the equal (=) sign.

For example, to calculate the cost of purchased discs in Sterling (£) in cell E3, type the following formula in the **Formula** box:

=C3*D3/100

	A	B	C
1			
2			
3		▨	

Word performs mathematical calculations on numbers in cells and inserts the result of the calculation as a field in the cell that contains the insertion pointer. Cells are referred to as A1, A2, B1, B2, and so on, with the letter representing a column and the number representing a row. Thus, B3 refers to the hatched cell.

When you use the **Table, Formula** command, Word assumes addition, unless you indicate otherwise, and proposes a sum based on the following rules:

- If the cell that contains the insertion pointer is at the intersection of a row and column and both contain numbers, Word sums the column. To sum the row, type =SUM(LEFT) or =SUM(RIGHT) in the **Formula** box, depending on the location of the insertion pointer.

- If the cell that contains the insertion pointer contains text or numbers, they are ignored.

- Word evaluates numbers beginning with the cell closest to the cell that contains the insertion pointer and continues until it reaches either a blank cell or a cell that contains text.

- If the numbers you are calculating include a number format, such as a £ sign, the result will also contain that format.

Fill in the rest of column E, then to calculate the total cost, place the insertion pointer in cell E9 and use the **Table, Formula** command. Word analyses your table and suggests the following function:

```
=SUM(ABOVE)
```

which is the correct formula in this case. On pressing **OK**, Word calculates the result and places it in cell E9. The completed table should look as follows:

Types of Removable Discs				
Description	Capacity Kbytes	Price/Unit Pence	Number Bought	Cost in £
Double-sided floppies	360	40	20	8
High-density floppies	1,200	60	40	24
Double-sided stiffies	720	80	60	48
High-density stiffies	1,440	100	80	80
Removable hard discs	105,000	6500	1	65
			Total	225

As the result of a calculation is inserted as a field in the cell that contains the insertion pointer, if you change the contents of the referenced cells, you must update the calculation. To do this, select the field (the cell that contains the formula) and press the **F9** function key.

In a formula you can specify any combination of mathematical and logical operators from the following list.

Addition	+
Subtraction	−
Multiplication	*
Division	/
Percent	%
Powers and roots	^
Equal to	=
Less than	<
Less than or equal to	<=
Greater than	>
Greater than or equal to	>=
Not equal to	< >

The following functions can accept references to table cells:

ABS( )	AND( )	AVERAGE( )
COUNT( )	DEFINED( )	FALSE( )
IF( )	INT( )	MAX( )
MIN( )	MOD( )	NOT( )
OR( )	PRODUCT( )	ROUND( )
SIGN( )	SUM( )	TRUE( )

The main reason for using formulae in a table, instead of just typing in the numbers, is that formulae will still give the correct final answer even if some of the data is changed. In this case you simply correct the data cells and Word recalculates the result once you update the field by pressing **F9**.

Editing a Table:

You can edit a table by inserting or deleting columns or rows, merging cells, or splitting a table.

To insert a row or column: Select where you want the new row or column to appear, remembering that the selected row (or column) and all rows below (or columns to its right) will move down (or to the right). Then you use the **Table, Insert Cells, Insert Entire Row** (or **Column**) command.

To delete a row or column: Select the row(s) or column(s) you want to delete, then use the **Table, Delete Cells, Delete Entire Row** (or **Column**) command.

To merge cells: Select the cells you want to merge, then use the **Table, Merge Cells** command. This command can be used to merge several cells to provide room for a table heading.

To split a table: Move the insertion pointer to where you want to split the table, then use the **Table, Split Cells** command. A blank line appears above the current row in the table, splitting it into two separate tables.

Formatting a Table:

You can enhance the looks of a table by selecting one of several pre-defined styles. To do this, place the insertion pointer in a cell of your table and use the **Table, Table AutoFormat** command. Select Classic 2 from the **Formats** list, to produce the display below and save it as **TABLE 1**.

Description	Capacity Kbytes	Price/Unit Pence	Number Bought	Cost in £
Double-sided floppies	360	40	20	8
High-density floppies	1,200	60	40	24
Double-sided stiffies	720	80	60	48
High-density stiffies	1,440	100	80	80
Removable hard discs	105,000	6500	1	65
			Total	225

Using Microsoft Graph

To chart your Word data, you can use Microsoft Graph 5.0, which is a separate program from Word. However, the program is designed to work with Word because it supports OLE (Object Linking and Embedding - see Chapter 10).

You can activate Graph by using the **Insert, Object** command and selecting 'Microsoft Graph' from the list in the Object dialogue box, shown below:

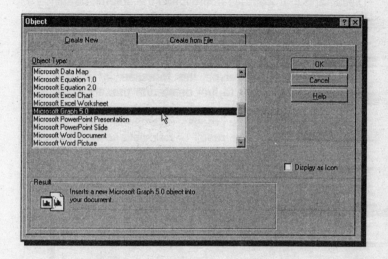

Microsoft Graph opens in an application window on top of Word, with default data in its data sheet. To change this default chart, you must change the data in the default data sheet. This can be done in various ways, but the easiest way is to either type your data directly into the displayed data sheet, or select the data from a Word table before activating Graph.

To demonstrate the way in which you can chart data held in a Word table, open the **TABLE 1** and then use your editing skills to first remove the AutoFormatting, then transform the table to what is displayed overleaf.

Removable Discs	Price p/Unit	No. Bought	Cost in £
Double-sided floppies	40	20	8.00
High-density floppies	60	40	24.00
Double-sided stiffies	80	60	48.00
High-density stiffies	100	80	80.00

Note that we have replaced 'Description' with 'Removable Discs', and that we have abbreviated the column headings so that they fit on one line. Also, we have deleted the column dealing with 'Capacity KBytes' and the row dealing with removable hard discs. However, having deleted a column, and in order to change the format of the 'Cost' column to currency, you must retype the formulae in what is now column D. Remember to first delete the present contents of column D.

Below, we show the process of entering the appropriate formula in cell D5. The result of calculations was formatted by selecting one from the **Number Format** list of the Formula dialogue box, as shown here.

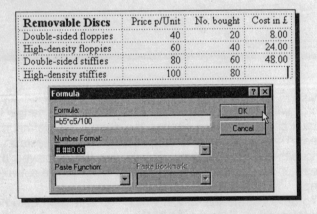

Save the resultant work as **TABLE 2**. Then select the table, by either highlighting it, or using the **Table, Select Table** command, and activate Microsoft Graph. If you don't select a table, Graph displays its default table and chart, as follows:

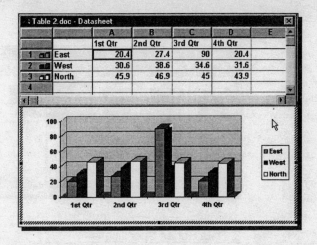

The ChartWizard:

If you select the table, the ChartWizard takes over, allowing you to tell Microsoft Graph how your data series is structured in the 3rd displayed dialogue box. The ChartWizard opens 4 dialogue boxes altogether, as follows:

1. Chart Type Selection

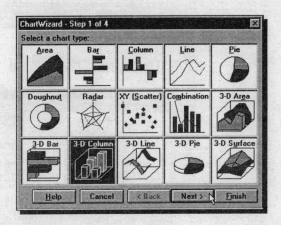

2. Format Selection for Chosen Chart

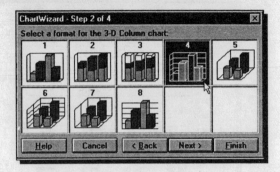

3. Data Series Specification

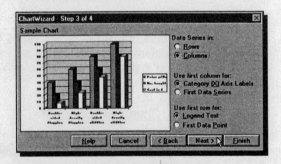

4. Legend and Title Selection

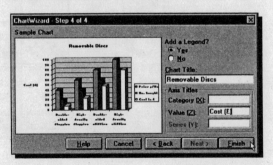

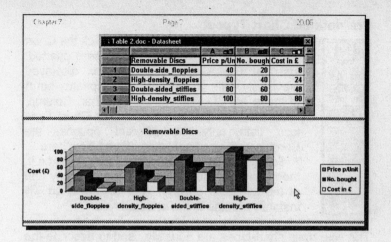

Removable Discs	Price p/Unit	No. bought	Cost in £
1 Double-side_floppies	40	20	8
2 High-density_floppies	60	40	24
3 Double-sided_stiffies	80	60	48
4 High-density_stiffies	100	80	80

Note: To display the captions in column A as the x-axis labels in their entirety, all spaces must be replaced with an underscore (the <Shift+–> key combination). This editing can be carried out on the Datasheet window by double-clicking each cell of column A and replacing the space with the underscore.

When you click outside the graph area, the chart is embedded in your Word document. Word will then include your chart within a frame and place it under the table containing the data from which it was drawn.

To access Microsoft Graph double-click at the frame containing your chart. Microsoft Graph will be activated with the chart ready for further work.

Warning: While working with Microsoft Graph a major program error occurred which prevented us not only from exiting Word, but also from shutting down our computer. The Help facility suggests that "you might need to reinstall the OLE application that you want to use" (as if expected), followed by a convoluted way of doing it!

If this happens to you, switch off your PC, then switch it on again and use the **Start, Setting, Control Panel** command, double-click the Add/Remove Program icon, select the application and remove it. Then reinstall the application.

Pre-defined Chart Types:

To select a different type of chart, click the Chart Type icon on the Toolbar, shown here opened. The 1st ChartWizard dialogue box displayed previously, lists 15 different chart options, but 6 of these are 3D versions of Area, Bar, Column, Line, Pie, and Surface charts. The Chart Type icon lists only 14 different options, the Combination chart not being offered from here.

To change an existing chart, double-click on it, then click the Chart Type icon and click any one of the available options. Your current chart will instantly change to the selected type.

The nine main chart-types are normally used to describe the following relationships between data:

Area: for showing a volume relationship between two series, such as production or sales, over a given length of time.

Bar: for comparing differences in data - non-continuous data that are not related over time - by depicting changes in horizontal bars to show positive and negative variations from a given position.

Column: for comparing separate items - non-continuous data which are related over time - by depicting changes in vertical bars to show positive and negative variations from a given position.

Line: for showing continuous changes in data with time.

Pie: for comparing parts with the whole. You can use this type of chart when you want to compare the percentage of an item from a single series of data with the whole series.

Doughnut: for comparing parts with the whole. Similar to pie charts, but can depict more than one series of data.

Radar: for plotting one series of data as angle values defined in radians, against one or more series defined in terms of a radius.

XY: for showing scatter relationships between X and Y. Scatter charts are used to depict items which are not related over time.

Combination: for comparing different chart types or different scaling systems by overlaying different type of charts (up to a maximum of four).

You can change the type of chart by selecting one of the fifteen alternate chart types (including the 3D variations of Area, Bar, Column, Line, Pie, and Surface) from the 1st ChartWizard dialogue box, pressing the **Next** button and choosing one of the pre-defined charts from the displayed selection, provided your data fits the selection.

Improving a Microsoft Chart:

A Microsoft Chart can be improved by using the Microsoft Draw facility. Double-click the chart, then click the Drawing icon on the Toolbar, which causes the Drawing Toolbar to be displayed, as shown below.

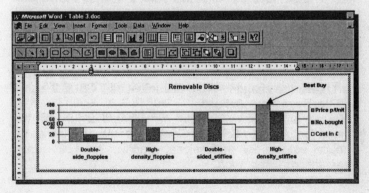

We have used the Arrow and Text Box buttons on the Drawing Toolbar to point to and annotate the 'best buy'. Since each value in the data used to create the chart, is a separate object within the chart, it can be moved, modified, or formatted. For example, double-clicking the chart title, or using the **Format, Font** command, displays the following dialogue box.

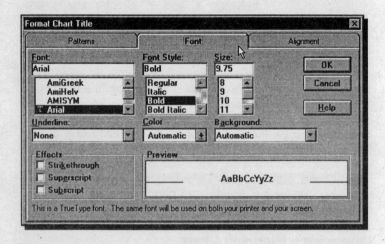

From here, you can change the Patterns, Font, and Alignment of the selected object.

Note: It is perhaps useful at this point to look at the various sub-menu options available under the main menu when a chart is selected. Everything in the sub-menu options has changed to a function dealing with a chart - try it.

When you have carried out all the required changes to your chart, save the changed Word document as **TABLE 3**, using the **File, Save As** command.

We are sure that you will get many hours of fun with the various features of Microsoft Graph and, more to the point, produce some very professional graphics for your report presentations within Word.

9. MANAGING LARGE DOCUMENTS

Many users' needs might demand that they work with either large documents, or with documents which are split into many files; they might even have to automate certain routines. In such cases, knowing something about outlines, file management and design of macros is imperative.

Outline Mode

Outline mode provides a way of viewing and organising the contents of a document. Nine outline levels can be used and these could be based on formatted headings (Heading 1, Heading 2, through to Heading 8), plus Normal text. By assigning each heading level a different paragraph style, it allows easy assimilation of the contents of a document.

The following display shows part of the first page of Chapter 1 of this book in the Normal editing view.

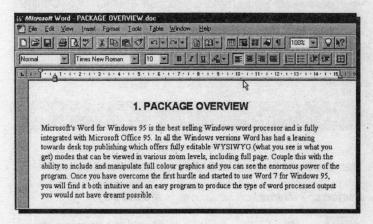

The same chapter is shown on the next page in outline view by either pressing the Outline button on the scroll bar, or selecting the **View, Outline** command. However, before you can see exactly what is shown here, you must assign styles to the various Headings. This can be done by selecting the outline view and assigning heading levels to your work using the tools on the outline bar which replaces the ruler.

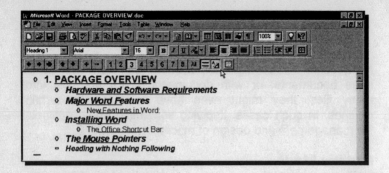

The actual formatting can only be seen if the Show Formatting icon (the one pointed to) is clicked.

Assigning Outline Levels:

'Outline' levels are stored as part of the formatting information in the paragraph styles, so you must assign these levels to your paragraph styles before you can usefully use 'Outline' mode. Then your outline will automatically display your document headings at the correct levels. This is an easy process carried out by selecting an existing heading and clicking one of the following buttons in the outline bar:

The name and function of these buttons is listed below.

Buttons	Name	Function
	Promote	Assigns heading to a higher outline level.
	Demote	Assigns to a lower outline level.
	Double Arrow	Demotes a heading to body text.

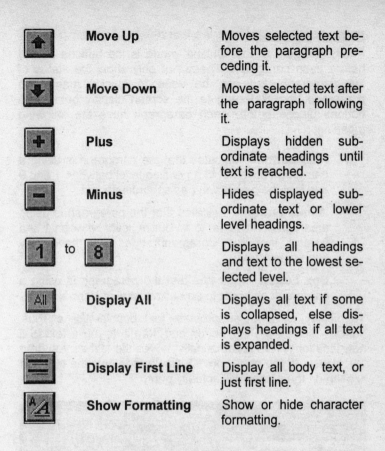

	Move Up	Moves selected text before the paragraph preceding it.
	Move Down	Moves selected text after the paragraph following it.
	Plus	Displays hidden subordinate headings until text is reached.
	Minus	Hides displayed subordinate text or lower level headings.
1 to 8		Displays all headings and text to the lowest selected level.
	Display All	Displays all text if some is collapsed, else displays headings if all text is expanded.
	Display First Line	Display all body text, or just first line.
	Show Formatting	Show or hide character formatting.

Using the expand and collapse commands, you can display the entire document or only selected text. Editing a document in 'Outline' mode is simple because you can control the level of detail that displays and quickly see the structure of the document. If you want to focus on the main topics in the document, you can collapse the text to display only paragraph styles set to high outline levels. If you want to view additional detail, you can expand the text to display text using paragraph styles set to lower outline levels.

Outline Buttons:

Another feature of the 'Outline' mode is the buttons placed before each paragraph. These not only show the status of the paragraph, but can be used to quickly manipulate paragraph text. Referring to the screen display below, the buttons placed before each paragraph have the following meaning:

✦ **Plus button** - Indicates that the paragraph is using a paragraph style set to an outline level between 1 and 9 and that the paragraph has subordinate text.

▭ **Minus button** - Indicates that the paragraph is using a paragraph style set to an outline level between 1 and 9 and that the paragraph does not have any subordinate text.

▫ **Box button** - Indicates that the paragraph is using a paragraph style set to an outline level of Normal text.

To display, or hide, subordinate text double-click a 'Plus' button. Click on a 'Plus' button and drag it, to move text to a new location. Word automatically moves the text as you drag the mouse. If you print from 'Outline' mode only the text that is seen on the screen will actually print.

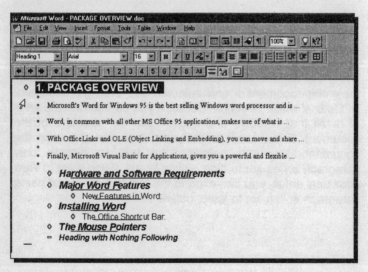

Outline Numbering:

If you want all your paragraphs numbered, you must rank all the styles and then assign one of the numbering schemes in the dialogue box obtained with the use of the **Format, Bullets and Numbering** command, and click the **Numbered** tab to obtain the dialogue box shown below.

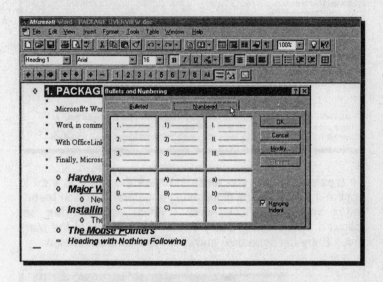

You could, of course, select the **Bulleted** tab, if you prefer.

Creating Table of Contents or an Index:

To create a table of contents, position the insertion point where you want the table of contents to appear, and use the

Insert, Index and Tables command, then click the **Table of Contents** tab to display the dialogue box shown here.

125

On pressing **OK** the table of contents is formed, as shown below, ready for you to format to your requirements.

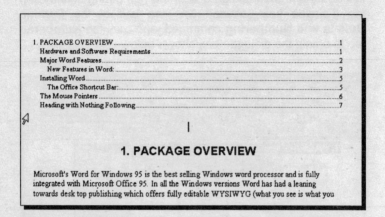

To create an index, you must first mark the text you want to appear in the index by highlighting it, before using the **Insert, Index and Tables** command. Then press the **Index** tab, followed by the **Mark Entry** button which displays the Mark Index Entry dialogue box, shown on the composite below.

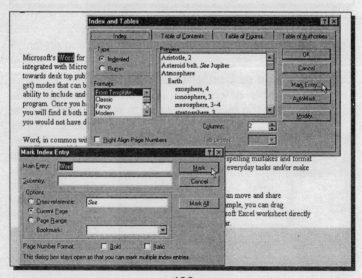

126

File Management

You can manage your documents from the **Open** menu option. First, you locate your file (you can even use wildcard characters in the **File name** box), then when the file is found, you select it and click the right mouse button to display the shortcut menu shown on the screen dump below. The shortcut menu contains all the commands you would ever need to manage your documents.

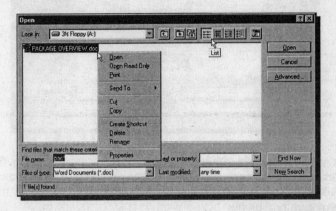

If more than one file is found, the first file is normally highlighted. If you click the **Details** button, shown below, full details on the listed files are displayed.

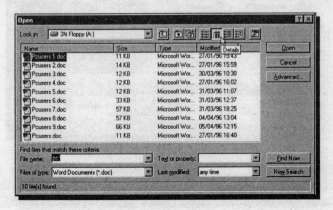

Finally, if you click the **Preview** button, shown below, you can see a preview of your document in the Preview box. As you select another file from the list, Word displays its contents too.

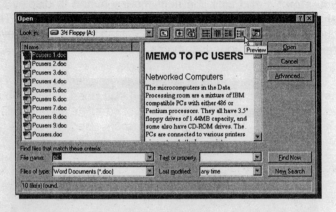

You can change what is shown in the above listing by pressing the **Commands and Settings** button and selecting **Sorting** from the displayed list of commands shown in the dialogue box below.

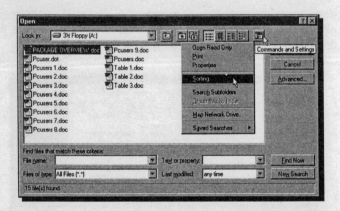

From this box, you can select one of the **Sort files by** options, to have files listed in **Ascending** or **Descending** order by 'File name', 'Size', 'Files of type', or 'Last modified'.

Assembling a Master Document

If you are involved in writing long documents, such as books, it is best if you split each document into sections (or chapters) of approximately 20 pages long. Anything above this length, particularly if it contains graphics, will strain your computer's resources. How much strain is experienced depends on how fast your computer is and how much Random Access Memory (RAM) it contains. In any case, large files take longer to open and save.

Having broken a long document into smaller sections you can work with these separately until you need to print your work in its entirety, or create a table of contents and an index with the page numbers. You will then need to create a 'Master Document'.

One method of doing this is to open a new document in Word, then use the **View, Master Document** command which will display the Master Document toolbar. Next, press the 'Insert Subdocument' button on the toolbar and select the file you want to insert into your Master Document (last file first), as shown below.

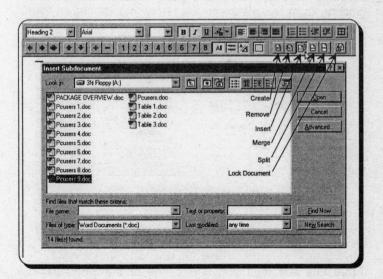

Printing a Master Document:

When you are finally ready to print the Master Document to paper, you can do so in two ways. To print the entire Master Document, print it from Normal view. To print only the outline of the Master Document, print it from Master Document view.

You could, of course, control the amount of detail you print by expanding or collapsing headings to display as much of the document as you require.

10. INSERTING INFORMATION

You can link or embed into Word, all or part of an existing file created either in a Microsoft Office application or in any other application that supports Object Linking and Embedding (OLE). However, if an application does not support OLE, then you must use the copy/cut and paste commands to copy or move information from such an application to Word.

In general, you copy, move, link or embed information depending on the imposed situation, as follows:

Imposed Situation	Method to Adopt
Inserted information into Word will not need updating, or Source application does not support OLE.	Copy or move
Inserted information needs to be automatically updated in the Word document as changes are made to the data in the source file, or Source file will always be available and you want to minimise the size of the Word document, or Source file is to be shared amongst several users.	Link
Inserted information into Word might need to be updated but source file might not be always accessible, or Word document needs to be edited without having these changes reflected in the source file.	Embed

Copying or Moving Information

To copy or move information into Word from programs running under Windows, such as Microsoft Office applications, is extremely easy. To move information, use the drag and drop facility, while to copy information, use the **Edit, Copy** and **Edit, Paste** commands.

To illustrate the technique, you will need to either create an Excel file, or have such a file on disc (see also 'Insert an Excel Worksheet in Word'). We will copy into Word our created Excel file **PROJECT.XLS**, considering the following two possibilities:

Source File Available without Application:

Let us assume that you only have the source file **PROJECT.XLS** on disc, but not the application that created it (that is you don't have Excel). In such a situation, you can only copy the contents of the whole file to the destination (in our case Word). To achieve this, do the following:

- Start Word and minimise it on the Taskbar.

- Use My Computer (or Explorer) to locate the file whose contents you want to copy into Word.

- Click the filename that you want to copy, hold the mouse button down and point to Word on the Taskbar until the application opens.

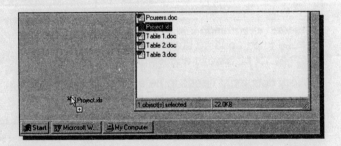

- While still holding the mouse button down, move the mouse pointer into Word's open document to the exact point where you would like to insert the contents of **PROJECT.XLS**.

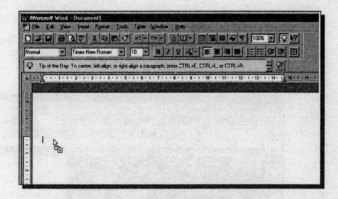

- Release the mouse button to place the contents of **PROJECT.XLS** into Word at that point.

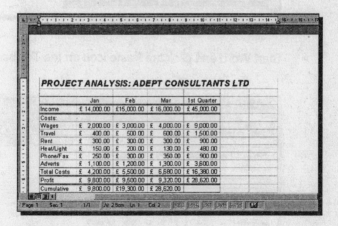

Source File and Application Available:

Assuming that you have both the file and the application that created it on your computer, you can copy all or part of the contents of the source file into a Word document. To achieve this, do the following:

- Start Excel and open **PROJECT.XLS**.

- Highlight as much information as you would like to copy and click the copy icon on the Toolbar.

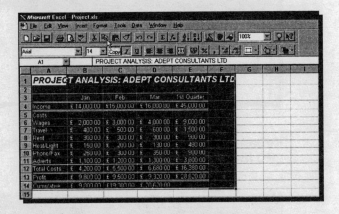

- Start Word and click the Paste icon on the Toolbar.

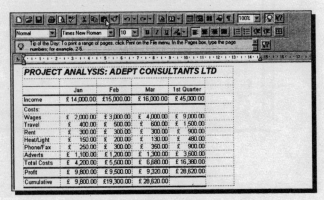

Insert an Excel Worksheet in Word

If the 'Insert Excel Worksheet' button, shown here, appears

 on your Word's Toolbar, you can use it to insert a worksheet of the required number of rows and columns, by simply clicking the button and dragging down to the right. As you drag the mouse, the 'Worksheet' button expands to create the grid of rows and columns, shown below, in a similar manner to that of creating rows and columns of tables.

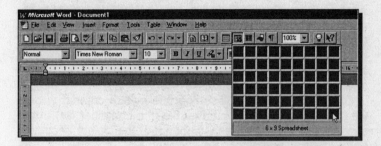

When you release the mouse button, the worksheet is inserted in your Word document. You can then insert data and apply functions to them, as shown below.

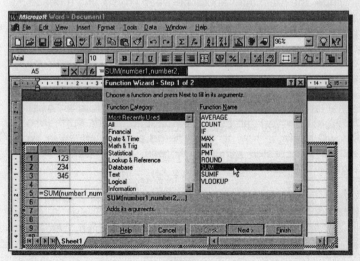

Object Linking and Embedding

Object Linking is copying information from one file (the source file) to another file (the destination file) and maintaining a connection between the two files. When information in the source file is changed, then the information in the destination file is automatically updated. Linked data is stored in the source file, while the file into which you place the data stores only the location of the source and displays a representation of the linked data.

For example, you would use Object Linking if you would want an Excel chart included in, say, a Word document to be updated whenever you changed the information used to create the chart in the first place within Excel. In such a case, the Excel worksheet containing the chart would be referred to as the source file, while the Word document would be referred to as the destination file.

Object Embedding is inserting information created in one file (the source file) into another file (the container file). After such information has been embedded, the object becomes part of the container file. When you double-click an embedded object, it opens in the application in which it was created in the first place. You can then edit it in place, and the original object in the source application remains unchanged.

Thus, the main differences between linking and embedding are where the data is stored and how it is updated after you place it in your file. Linking saves you disc space as only one copy of the linked object is kept on disc. Embedding a logo chosen for your headed paper, saves the logo with every saved letter!

In what follows, we will discuss how you can link or embed either an entire file or selected information from an existing file, and how you can edit an embedded object. Furthermore, we will examine how to mail merge a letter written in Word with a list created either in Access, Excel, Schedule+, or even Word itself.

To insert a single address into a Word letter from Schedule+, click the 'Insert Address' button on the Toolbar, shown here, and select a name from the drop-down menu.

Embedding a New Object:

To embed a new object into an application, do the following:

- Open the container file, say Word, and click where you want to embed the new object.

- Use the **I**nsert, **O**bject command, to open the Object dialogue box, shown below, when the **C**reate New tab is clicked.

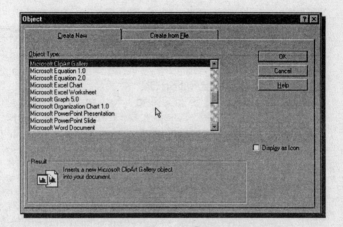

Note that only applications which are installed on your computer and support linking and embedding appear in the **O**bject Type box.

- In the **O**bject Type box, click the type of object you want to create, and press **OK**.

As an example, we selected Microsoft ClipArt (you could select a different application) which opens the Microsoft ClipArt Gallery from which we selected the object shown here. Pressing the **I**nsert button on the ClipArt application, embeds the object within Word. Double-clicking on such an object, opens up the original application.

Linking or Embedding an Existing File:

To embed an existing file in its entirety into a Word document, do the following:

- Open the Word document, and click where you want to embed the file.

- Use the **Insert, Object** command, to open the Object dialogue box, shown below, when the **Create from File** tab is clicked.

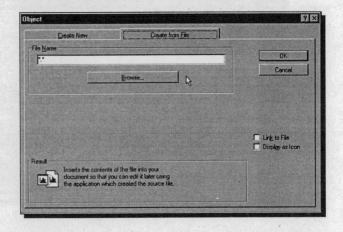

To locate the file you want to link or embed, click **Browse**, and then select the options you want.

- In the **File Name** box, type the name of the file you want to link or embed.

- To maintain a link to the original file, check the **Link to File** box.

Note: To insert graphics files, use the **Insert, Picture** command instead of the **Insert, Object** command. This opens up the Insert Picture dialogue box which allows you to specify within a **Look in** box the folder and file you want to insert.

Linking or Embedding Selected Information:

To link or embed selected information from an existing file created in one application into Word, do the following:

- Select the information in the source file you want to link or embed.

- Use the **Edit, Copy** command to copy the selected information to the Clipboard.

- Switch to the Word document in which you want to place the information, and then click where you want the information to appear.

- Use the **Edit, Paste Special** command to open the following dialogue box:

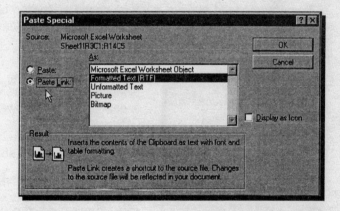

- To link the information, click the **Paste Link** radio button, or to embed the information, click the **Paste** radio button. In the **As** box, click the item with the word 'Object' in its name. For example, if you copied the information from an Excel worksheet, as we have for this example, the Formatted Text (RTF) appears in the **As** box. Select this entry and press **OK**.

Editing an Embedded Object:

If the application in which you created an embedded object is installed on your computer, double-click the object to open it for editing. Some applications start the original application in a separate window and then open the object for editing, while other applications temporarily replace the menus and toolbars in the current application so that you can edit the embedded object in place, without switching to another window.

If the application in which an embedded object was created is not installed on your computer, convert the object to the file format of an application you do have. For example, if your Word document contains an embedded Microsoft Works Spreadsheet object and you do not have Works, you can convert the object to an Excel Workbook format and edit it in Excel.

Some embedded objects, such as sound and video clips, when double-clicked start playing their contents, instead of opening an application for editing.

For example, copying the Goodtime video icon from its folder in the Windows 95 CD into Word and double-clicking the icon, starts the video, as shown here.

To edit one of these objects, select it and use the **Edit, {Video Clip} Object, Edit** command. What appears within the curly brackets here depends on the selected object; video clip in this case.

Of course, unless you have the facilities required for editing such objects, you will be unable to do so.

140

Mail Merging Lists

There are times when you may want to send the same basic letter to several different people, or companies. The easiest way to do this is with a Merge operation. Two files are prepared; a 'Data' file with the names and addresses, and a 'Form' file, containing the text and format of the letter. The two files are then merged together to produce a third file containing an individual letter to each party listed in the original data file.

Before creating a list of names and addresses for a mail merge, you need to select the Office application that is most suited to the task. For a mail merge, you can use a list you create in Access, Excel, Schedule+, or Microsoft Word.

- For a long list in which you expect to add, change, or delete records, and for which you want powerful sorting and searching capabilities at your disposal, you should use either Access or Excel, then specify the appropriate data file in the Word Mail Merge Helper (see below).

- To use the list of names and addresses in your Schedule+ Contact List, you select this list in the Word Mail Merge Helper.

- For a small to medium size list of names and addresses in which you do not expect to make many changes, you could select to create a list in the Word Mail Merge Helper.

The Word Mail Merger Helper is a dialogue box in which you specify:

(a) whether you want to create form letters, labels, or print envelopes,

(b) where your list of names and addresses (data) is to be found, and

(c) what query options are to be applied to your data list before the merging process starts.

These will be explained next with illustrated examples.

We will illustrate the merge procedure by using a memo created in Word (**PCUSERS 1**) and a table which can be created in Word, or already exists either in an electronic book such as Schedule+, in Excel or in an Access table.

No matter which method you choose, first start Word and open the **PCUSERS 1** memo (or your own letter), then provide two empty lines at the very top of the memo/letter by placing the insertion pointer at the beginning of the memo and pressing <Enter> twice. Then select these two empty lines and choose the Normal paragraph style.

Next, select **Tools, Mail Merge** which displays the Mail Merge Helper dialogue box shown below.

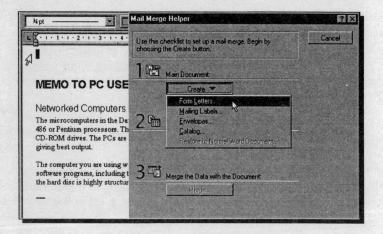

In this box, you define in three successive steps:

1. The document to be used,
2. The source of your data, and
3. The merging of the two.

Start by clicking the **Create** button, select the **Form Letters** option, and click the **Active Window** button.

Next, click the **<u>G</u>et Data** button which causes a drop-down menu to display, shown below.

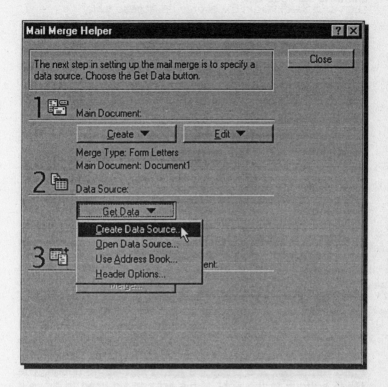

It is from this menu that you can select either to create your data source (the list of addresses) in Word, open (or import) an existing list of addresses which might be found in either Word, Excel, Access, etc., or use a list of contacts in an electronic address book such as Schedule+.

In what follows, we will examine each of these options (in the same order as the list in the above drop-down menu). You can, of course, skip the Create an Address List in Word section, if you already have an existing data list.

Creating an Address List in Word:

Selecting the **Create Data Source** menu option, displays the following dialogue box.

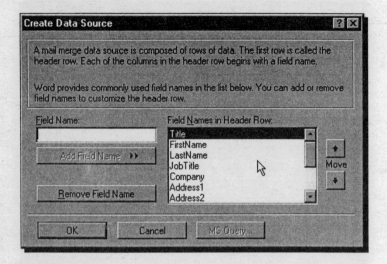

As you can see, Word provides commonly used field names for your address list. Unwanted field names can be deleted from the list by selecting them and pressing the **Remove Field Name** button. To add your own field name, type it in the **Field Name** box and press the **Add Field Name** button. The **Move** buttons to the right of the list can be used to move a selected field in the list to the top or bottom of the list by pressing the up-arrow or down-arrow, respectively.

Having compiled the required field names for your list, pressing the **OK** button, displays a Save As dialogue box, in which you can name your data list, say **Address**. Word automatically adds the file extension **.doc**, and displays the following warning dialogue box which allows you to either edit the data source or the main document.

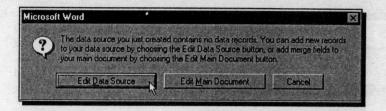

Press the **Edit Data Source** button if you want to create or edit your data list. Doing so displays the following Data Form dialogue box.

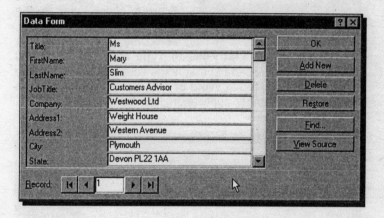

Here you can create a new data list or edit an existing one. We have typed in one fictitious entry in order to demonstrate the process, but we have not attempted to change the field names provided in any way whatsoever.

Having created a Word data list, added to one or edited one, pressing **OK** prompts you to save your changes to the already existing filename.

What follows is common to all existing data files, no matter in which application you chose to create it.

Getting an Address List:

If you have not done so already, open the letter you want to mail merge, place the cursor in the position you want the address to appear, and select **Tools, Mail Merge** in Word. Then press the **Create** button in the Mail Merge Helper and choose **Form Letters**, **Active Window**.

Next, click the **Get Data** button (the 2nd step in the Mail Merge Helper) which causes a drop-down menu, shown here, to display.

Select the **Open Data Source** option, and in the displayed dialogue box, select the drive, and click the down-arrow on the **List Files of Type** box. From here you can choose the type of file that holds your address list, which could be one created in Word or a text editor (or exported in that form from another application), or an Access file.

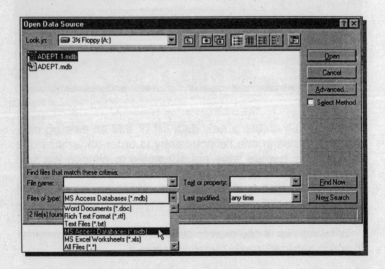

For our example we chose the **MS Access Database** type of file, which lists the databases on the specified drive and path.

Next, select the database that holds your address data and click the **OK** button. Access is then loaded and the tables within the selected database are listed. Microsoft Access then asks you to choose the Table that contains your data. Select the one that does, and click the **OK** button.

At this point, Microsoft Word displays a warning message, shown below, to the effect that no merge fields have been found on your document.

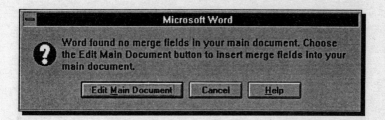

Don't worry about this, as we will rectify this omission, as follows:

- Click the **Edit Main Document** button on the above warning box which displays your document with an additional toolbar below the Formatting bar, as shown below.

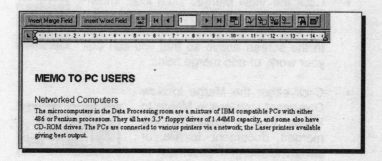

- Click the **Insert Merge Field** button on the new toolbar. This displays the fields in your selected Access table that contains your addresses.

147

- Select in turn, the fields you want to use. To place these on the document on separate lines, press <Enter> after each selection. To place others on the same line, press the space bar after each selection.

The first few lines of your document could look as follows (we have typed in the word FAO: on the last line of the address, before inserting the 'Contact' field.

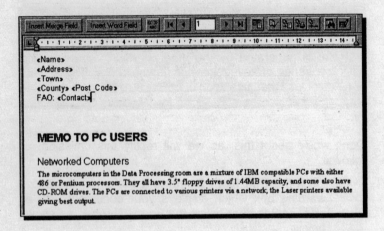

- Click the View Merged Data icon, shown to the right, to see your merged data. Clicking this icon once more, returns you to the screen above so that you can edit your work, or add merge fields.

- Click either the Merge to New Document icon or the Merge to Printer icon to create a new merged document to file or send the merged document to the printer.

That's all there is to it. You will possibly find it takes as little time to do, as it did to read about it!

11. WORD MACROS

Word Macro Basics

A macro is simply a set of instructions made up of a sequence of keystrokes, mouse selections, or commands stored in a macro file. After saving, or writing, a macro and attaching a quick key combination to it, you can run the same sequence of commands whenever you want. This can save a lot of time and, especially with repetitive operations, can save mistakes creeping into your work.

In Word there are two basic ways of creating macros. The first one is generated by the program itself, recording and saving a series of keystrokes, or mouse clicks. The second one involves the use of WordBasic, the programming language that comes with Word for Windows 95. With this method, you can write quite complex macro programs directly into a macro file using the Word for Windows' macro editor.

Recording a Macro:

To demonstrate how easy it is to save and name a macro, we will start with a simplistic one that enhances the word at the cursor to bold type in italics. Open **PCUSERS 1**, place the cursor in a document word and either double-click the **REC** button on the Status bar, shown below, or select the **Tools**, **Macro** command and press the **Record** button on the displayed Macro dialogue box.

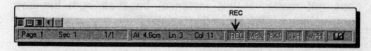

Either of these, opens the Record Macro dialogue box shown on the next page. In the **Record Macro Name** input box, type a name for your macro (call it Bolditlc), then give your macro a **Description** (such as Bold & Italic) and click on the **Keyboard** button. In the displayed Customize dialogue box, press a suitable key stroke combination, such as <Ctrl+Shift+I>, in the **Press New Shortcut Key** input box.

The shortcut key combination will appear in the input box and immediately below it you will be informed whether this key combination is currently attached to an internal macro or not, as shown below:

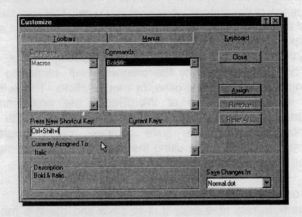

Most <Ctrl> or <Shift> keys with a letter or function key combinations are suitable (the word [Mark Citation] will appear under the **Currently Assigned To:** heading) if the chosen combination of keys is not already assigned to a macro. Our choice of key stokes results in the message 'Italic', under the **Currently Assigned To:** heading. This does not matter in this instance, because both the key combinations <Ctrl+I> and <Ctrl+Shift+I> are assigned to Italic, so we can use one. Finally, press the **Assign** button followed by the **Close** button.

From this point on, all key strokes and mouse clicks (but not mouse movements in the editing area) will be recorded. To indicate that the recorder is on, Word attaches a recorder graphic to the mouse pointer, as shown here. Word also displays the Stop and Pause buttons to allow you to stop or pause a macro.

150

A macro can also be stopped by double-clicking at the REC button on the Status bar.

While the cursor is still placed in the word to be modified, use the key strokes, <Ctrl+→> to move to the end of the current word, followed by <Shift+Ctrl+←>, to highlight the word, click the Bold and Italic buttons on the Formatting toolbar, press <→> to cancel the highlight and click the Stop button on the Macro Record toolbar. Your macro should now be recorded and held in memory.

Saving a Macro to Disc:

To save your macro to disc, use the **File, Save As** command and give your macro the name **MACRO 1**. If you quit Word without saving the template, you will be asked if you want to save the changes made to the template. Choose the **Yes** button to save your macro.

Playing Back a Macro:

There are four main ways of running a macro. You can use the playback shortcut keys straight from the keyboard; in our case place the cursor in another word and press <Ctrl+Shift+I>. The word should be enhanced automatically. If not, check back that you carried out the instructions correctly.

The second method is to select the **Tools**, **Macro** command, then select the macro from the list, as shown here, and press the **Run** button. From this dialogue box you can also **Edit**, **Delete**, or select the **Organizer** so that you can **Rename** macros.

The last two methods of activating a macro are to attach it to a custom button on a toolbar or a menu, and simply click the button or the menu option.

Attaching Macros to a Toolbar or a Menu:

To assign a macro to a toolbar or a menu, use the **Tools, Customize** command, and select **Macros** from the **Categories** list of the displayed dialogue box, shown below.

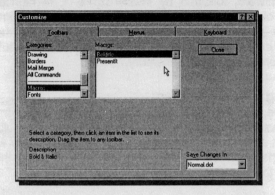

Next, click the macro from the **Macros** list to see its description and drag the macro name to any button on the toolbars. The selected macro replaces the original function of the button.

To assign a macro to a menu, click the **Menus** tab of the Customize dialogue box, select **Macros** from the **Categories** list on the displayed dialogue box, shown on the bottom half of the next page, and press the **Add** button. Next, click the **Menu Bar** button, type an entry in the **Name on Menu Bar** input box. Finally, select the **Position on Menu Bar** on which the entry should appear.

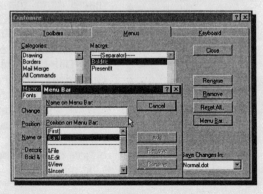

Editing a Macro:

You can edit the entries in a macro file by selecting the **Tools**, **Macros**, command which opens the Macro dialogue box in which you select the macro file to edit. Select the 'Bolditlc' file, assuming of course that you saved it with that name, and press the **Edit** button. Word loads the file into the normal editing screen and you treat the macro file exactly the same as any other. The listing of our Bolditlc file should look as follows:

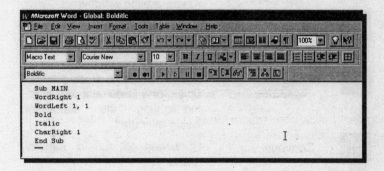

If you look at this listing you will see that it would be very easy to edit the commands in the file. If you do edit it, you should then save the file with the **File, Save All** command.

Notice the following two aspects in the screen display above:

(a) When editing a macro, the Ruler is replaced by a Macro Editing bar, and

(b) Macros within WordBasic are considered to be 'subroutines' that run under Word for Windows.

The buttons on the Macro Editing bar have the functions described on the next page.

Button	Name	Function
	Record	Displays the Record Macro dialogue box so that you can begin to record a macro.
	Record Next C'nd	Records the next command you choose and inserts the corresponding WordBasic instruction in the active macro-editing window.
	Start	Runs the active macro which must be opened in a macro-editing window.
	Trace	Runs the macro from start to finish, one statement at a time, highlighting the statement being executed.
	Continue	Continues to run a paused macro.
	Stop	Stops recording or running a macro.
	Step	Runs a macro one statement at a time, highlighting the statement and pausing until the Step button is pressed again.
	Step Subs	Executes the macro one subroutine at a time, highlighting the first line of the following subroutine and pausing until the Step Subs button is pressed again.
	Show Variables	Shows the current value of the variables used in the macro and allows you to reset these during macro execution.

Add/Remove REM Adds REM statements to or removes them from the selected lines in a macro-editing window. REM statements are ignored during macro execution.

 Macro Records a macro, runs any macro or standard Word command, or opens a macro for editing.

 Dialog Editor Starts the Dialog Editor, if it is not already running, and switches to it.

It is easy to make small changes to macros you have recorded using the buttons on the Macro Editing bar. However, if you wanted to create a macro that executed commands which could not be recorded, such as switching to a particular directory and displaying the Open dialogue box, then you must either learn to use Word's macro language, WordBasic or learn the programming language Visual Basic.

If you have installed the complete Word package, then WordBasic Help should have been installed. If that is the case, then you could view the on-line reference on WorldBasic by using the Answer Wizard, as follows:

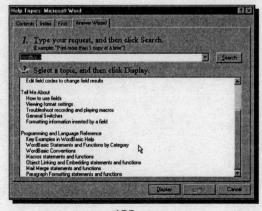

Within the listed help topics, you will find a wealth of information, showing how to program your macros and how to use the various built-in functions. Try it, you will learn a lot.

* * *

If you are interested in Visual Basic, may we suggest that you look at the book *Programming in Visual BASIC for Windows* (BP346), also published by BERNARD BABANI (publishing) Ltd.

* * *

APPENDIX A
WORD'S TOOLBAR BUTTONS

The Standard Toolbar Buttons:

The Standard Toolbar contains 22 buttons which have the following effect:

Button	Effect
	Creates a new document based on the NORMAL.DOT template.
	Opens an existing document or template.
	Saves the active document or template.
	Prints the active document using the current defaults.
	Prints a preview of the document on screen.
	Checks the spelling in the active document.
	Cuts the selection and puts it on the clipboard.
	Copies the selection and puts it on the clipboard.
	Pastes the clipboard contents at the insertion point.

Paints the format of a selection at the insertion point.

 Undoes the last action.

 Redoes the last action.

 AutoFormats selection.

 Inserts AutoText.

 Inserts a table.

 Insert a Microsoft Excel worksheet.

 Changes the column format within selected sections.

 Starts Microsoft Draw.

 Starts Microsoft Graph.

 Displays or hides special non-printing characters, such as tabs or hard returns.

 Scales the document to 100% in the normal view.

 Provides help on an item by pointing to it.

APPENDIX B
KEYBOARD SHORTCUTS

Shortcuts for Activating Commands:
To execute commands quickly, press the following key combinations:

Command	*Press*
To start a New document	Ctrl +N
To Open a document	Ctrl+O
To Save a document	Ctrl+S
To Print a document	Ctrl+P
To Undo an edit or command	Ctrl+Z
To Repeat Undo	Ctrl+Y
To Cut a selected block	Ctrl+X
To Copy a selected block	Ctrl+C
To Paste a cut or copied block	Ctrl+V
To Clear a selected block	Del
To Select All (entire document)	Ctrl+A
To Find specified text or formatting	Ctrl+F
To Find and Replace text or formatting	Ctrl+H
To Go To a specified page	Ctrl+G
To activate the Spelling tool	F7
To activate the Thesaurus tool	Shift+F7
To select a Table	Alt+5
(5 on the numeric keyboard)	

Shortcuts for Navigating and SelectingText:
You can move the cursor around a document with the normal direction keys, and with the key combinations shown below. To select text, press the <Shift> key and hold it pressed prior to using the navigational key combinations:

To Move	*Press*
Left one character	←
Right one character	→
Up one line	↑
Down one line	↓
Left one word	Ctrl+←
Right one word	Ctrl+→

To beginning of line	Home
To end of line	End
To paragraph beginning	Ctrl+↑
To paragraph end	Ctrl+↓
Up one screen	PgUp
Down one screen	PgDn
To top of previous page	Ctrl+PgUp
To top of next page	Ctrl+PgDn
To beginning of file	Ctrl+Home
To end of file	Ctrl+End

In a multi-page document, use <Ctrl+G> to jump to a specified page number.

Advanced Search Operators:

The list below gives the key combinations of special characters to type into the **Find What** and **Replace With** boxes when the **Use Pattern Matching** box is checked.

To find or replace	*Type*
Any single character within a pattern. For example, searching for nec?, will find neck, connect, etc.	?
Any string of characters. For example, searching for c*r, will find such words as cellar, chillier, etc., also parts of words such as character, and combinations of words such as connect, cellar.	*
One of the specified characters. For example, searching for d[oi]g, will find such words as dog and dig.	[ ]
Any single character in the specified range. For example, searching for [b-f]ore, will find such words as bore, core, fore, etc.	[-]
Any single character except the character inside the brackets. For example, searching for l[!o]ve, will find live, but not love.	[!]

Any single character except characters in the range inside the brackets. For example, searching for [!s-z]ong, will find long but not song.	[!s-z]
Exactly n occurrences of the previous character. For example, searching for me{2}t, will find meet but not met.	{n}
At least n occurrences of the previous character. For example, searching for me{1,}t, will find met and meet.	{n,}
From n to m occurrences of the previous character. For example, searching for 9{1,3}, will find 9, 99, and 999.	{n,m}
One or more occurrences of the previous character. For example, searching for ro@t, will find rot and root.	@
The beginning of a word. For example, searching for <on, will find on and onto, but not upon.	<
The end of a word. For example, searching for >on, will find on and upon, but not onto.	>

Text Formatting with Quick Keys:

To format selected text, use the following shortcut keys.

To Format	*Type*
Bold	Ctrl+B
Italic	Ctrl+I
Underline	Ctrl+U
Word underline	Ctrl+Shift+W
Double underline	Ctrl+Shift+D
Subscript	Ctrl+=
Superscript	Ctrl+Shift+=
Small caps	Ctrl+Shift+K

161

All caps	Ctrl+Shift+A
Change case letters	Shift+F3
Hide text	Ctrl+Shift+H
Copy formats	Ctrl+Shift+C
Paste formats	Ctrl+Shift+V
Remove formats	Ctrl+Space
Next larger font size	Ctrl+>
Next smaller font size	Ctrl+<

Paragraph Alignment Shortcuts:

You can align a paragraph at the left margin (the default), at the right margin, centred between both margins, or justified between both margins. This can be achieved as follows:

To Format	*Type*
Left align	Ctrl+L
Centre align	Ctrl+E
Right align	Ctrl+R
Justify	Ctrl+J
Indent from left margin	Ctrl+M
Decrease indent	Ctrl+Shift+M
Create a hanging indent	Ctrl+T
Decrease a hanging indent	Ctrl+Shift+T
Add or remove 12 points of space before a paragraph	Ctrl+0 (zero)
Remove paragraph formats not applied by a style	Ctrl+Q
Restore default formatting by applying the Normal style	Ctrl+Shift+N
Display or hide non-printing characters (such as · → ¶)	Ctrl+*

Paragraph Spacing Shortcuts:

To display a paragraph on screen or printed on paper in single-line, 1½-line, or double-line spacing, use the following:

To Format	*Type*
Single-spaced lines	Ctrl+1
One-and-a-half-spaced lines	Ctrl+5
Double-spaced lines	Ctrl+2

APPENDIX C
BUILDING EQUATIONS

As equation building is not everyone's cup of tea, we have consigned it to an appendix to avoid confusing non-scientists.

We assume here that you have used the **Insert, Object** command, and selected 'Microsoft Equation 2.0' from the **Object Type** list of the Object dialogue box, as discussed on page 88. When the Equation Editor is on your screen, pressing **F1**, displays a Help screen with several topics.

Selecting the first option, reveals a further list of topics, of which the most important to look-up first are: 'Equation Editor Basics' and 'Equation Editor, and what it can do'. The first tells you about the Equation Toolbar and how you can use it.

For example, the top row of the Equation Editor toolbar has buttons for inserting more than 150 mathematical symbols, many of which are not available in the standard Symbol font. To insert a symbol in an equation, click a button on the top row of the toolbar, as shown on the composite screen dump below, and then click the specific symbol from the palette that appears under the button.

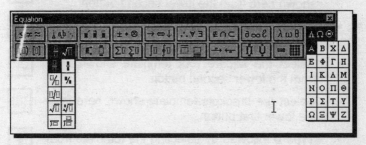

The bottom row of the Equation Editor toolbar has buttons for inserting templates or frameworks that contain such symbols as fractions, radicals, summations, integrals, products, matrices, and various fences or matching pairs of symbols such as brackets and braces. There are about 120 templates, grouped on palettes, many of which contain slots - spaces into which you type text and insert symbols. Templates can be nested, by inserting them in the slots of other templates, to build complex hierarchical formulae.

Finally, select the second recommended help topic to find out about spacing and alignment, expanding templates, styles, embellishments, and how to position the insertion pointer so that you can achieve best results.

As an example, we will take you through the steps required, when using the Equation Editor, to construct the equation for the solution of a quadratic equation. The required equation is:

$$x = \frac{-b \pm \sqrt{\{b^2 - 4ac\}}}{2a}$$

To construct this equation, place the insertion pointer at the required place in your document, activate the Equation Editor, and follow the steps listed below. The templates and symbols you require from the Equation Editor are shown to the right of the appropriate step.

- Type *x* = followed by selecting the template shown here from the lower second button.

- Type –*b* followed by selecting the ± symbol from the upper fourth button.

- Select the square root template shown here from the lower second button.

- Select the brackets template shown here from the lower first button.

- Type *b* followed by selecting the template from the lower third button.

- Type **2** and re-position the insertion pointer as shown here, and then type –*4ac*.

- Position the insertion pointer at the denominator and type *2a*.

Obviously, the Equation Editor is capable of a lot more than what we have covered here, but this simple example should serve to get you started. Try it, it's simpler than it looks.

INDEX

NOTES

174

COMPANION DISCS TO BOOKS

COMPANION DISCS are available for most books written by the same author(s) and published by BERNARD BABANI (publishing) LTD, as listed at the front of this book (except for those marked with an asterisk). These books contain many pages of file/program listings. There is no reason why you should spend hours typing them into your computer, unless you wish to do so, or need the practice.

COMPANION DISCS come in 3½" format with all example listings.

ORDERING INSTRUCTIONS

To obtain your copy of a companion disc, fill in the order form below or a copy of it, enclose a cheque (payable to **P.R.M. Oliver**) or a postal order, and send it to the address below. Make sure you fill in your name and address and specify the book number and title in your order.

Book No.	Book Name	Unit Price	Total Price
BP		£3.50	
BP		£3.50	
BP		£3.50	
Name		Sub-total	£.............
Address:		P & P (@ 45p/disc)	£.............
		Total Due	£.............
Send to: P.R.M. Oliver, CSM, Pool, Redruth, Cornwall, TR15 3SE			